Straight A's

If I Can Do It, So Can You

John C. Stowers, Jr., M.D.

McGraw-Hill, Inc.

New York   St. Louis   San Francisco   Auckland   Bogotá
Caracas   Lisbon   London   Madrid   Mexico City   Milan   Montreal
New Delhi   San Juan   Singapore   Sydney   Tokyo   Toronto

This book was set in New Century Schoolbook
by Ruttle, Shaw & Wetherill, Inc.
The editors were Tim Julet and David Dunham;
the designer was Karen K. Quigley;
the production supervisor was Annette Mayeski.
R. R. Donnelley & Sons Company was printer and
binder.

Straight A's: If I Can Do It, So Can You

This book is printed on acid-free paper.

2 3 4 5 6 7 8 9 0 DOC DOC 9 0 9 8 7 6

ISBN 0-07-061823-2 (text version)
ISBN 0-07-061824-0 (trade version)

Library of Congress Cataloging-in-Publication Data

Stowers, John C.
    Straight A's: if I can do it, so can you / John C. Stowers, Jr.
        p.   cm.
    Includes index.
    ISBN 0-07-061823-2 (text version).—ISBN 0-07-061824-0
        (trade version).
        1. College student orientation—Handbooks, manuals, etc.
    2. Study skills—Handbooks, manuals, etc.   I. Title.
    LB2343.3.S76   1996
    378.1'7'02812—dc20   95-784

Straight A's

If I Can Do It, So Can You

About the Author

Doctor Stowers, John to his readers and friends, has lived most of his life in northern California. At the age of 18 he took over the responsibilities of running his family's small business when his father passed away suddenly. During this time he enjoyed working in many community service projects and began to appreciate the importance of an education. His desire to further his education grew until finally he gave up the business and returned to college. In 1991 he graduated with a 3.96 grade-point average and highest honors in chemistry from Purdue University. He then accepted a position in medical school at the University of California, where he graduated with a Medical Degree in 1995. Currently he is completing a residency training program in Emergency Medicine, and always appreciates hearing from his readers and fellow students.

*This book is dedicated
to the memory of my father
who taught me to
never compromise my principles,
and to my mother
who gave me the confidence
to succeed.*

Contents

Chapter 9

Chapter 10

Chapter 11

Chapter 12

Chapter 13

Chapter 14

Chapter 15

Chapter 16

Special Topics: **135**

Introduction

Are you about to begin college and determined to do well? Already enrolled and worried about the challenges you're facing? Somewhere along the road toward your degree and panicking about your grades? This book is for you. It's for everyone who wants to succeed in college.

This book is a student-written study guide; it's the study guide I wish I had when I began college. It provides you with the comprehensive approach to study that I developed after facing the hard reality of either improving my grades or giving up my dream of becoming a physician. You'll learn about the importance of believing in yourself and your ability to be a straight-"A" student. I'll tell you how to approach your instructors and about the role classmates will play in your college career. Grading systems, special tips for part-time students, how to register for classes, and stress management are discussed. But the bulk of the book is devoted to managing your studies before, during, and after class; to optimizing your use of time; to tailoring your studying to specific types of classes; and to preparing for and taking exams. My advice is specific and detailed, and my study tips are based on my own experience and the experiences of the many other straight-"A" students and helpful instructors with whom I talked before writing this book.

I tell my story in Chapter 1, but let me say here: I wasn't a straight-"A" student in college because my IQ was exceptionally high. I was able to do so well in college because I followed the study methods I've spelled out in this book. I'm confident that you can also achieve your academic goals. Happy reading and good luck!

John C. Stowers, Jr.

Acknowledgments

Special thanks to Carolyn Kroehler, a very talented writer and friend, without whose help this book would not exist in its present form. To my wife Shari L. Stowers, Paul Coelho, M.D., and Daniel E. Andrews, M.D., for their support and friendship. And, to the following top professors/educators whom I've had the privilege to learn from: William J. King, M.S., Terry L. Shell, M.S., Anthony A. Taylor, M.S., Ronald A. Head, M.S., Richard Frey, M.S., Gregory M. Novak, Ph.D., Gordon Fricke, Ph.D., Martin Bard, Ph.D., and Richard Wyma, Ph.D.

I would also like to thank the following reviewers for their many helpful comments and suggestions: Ronald B. Adler, Santa Barbara City College; Santi Buscemi, Middlesex County College; Johnine Callahan, Grand Valley State University; Roger Callanan, North Carolina State University; Barbara Clouse, Youngstown State University; Greg Clouse, Liberty High School; Richard Conway, Nassau Community College; Gerald L. Giles, Salt Lake Community College; Mike Jaromin, SUNY, Albany; Emily Mead, Cornell University; Paula Rivard, Middlesex County College; and Tracey Sciuto, Stonehill College.

John C. Stowers, Jr.

1

If I Can Do It,
So Can You

I am not a genius. In fact, I was a mediocre high school student. I spent the first four years after high school working in my dad's typewriter repair business. And when I finally did go to college, my first semester was a big disappointment.

But I figured out, mostly by talking to top students, how to do well in college. And after that first semester, I got nothing but A's. Now I'm in a top medical school, with a full scholarship.

If I can do it, you can too. The purpose of this book is to tell you how.

WHY DID I WRITE THIS BOOK?

When I was about to graduate, I was approached by one of my science instructors at Purdue University and asked to consider writing a paper on how to get A's. My professor said most incoming college students aren't prepared for college work, and most colleges don't offer much in the way of assistance. Maybe a student-written guide would help students get good grades.

Why was I singled out among all the students in my graduating class to write such a paper? Because I had learned the hard way how to get good grades. As a high school student, I saw no future in school and had no plans to go to college. I never studied and spent most of my four years playing sports and building farm equipment in the Ag shop. I finished in the middle of my class with a B average, and I received D's in math. I did go on to college, but one month into my first semester my father died, so I dropped out of school to take over his typewriter repair business. Four years later, when I decided I wanted to be a doctor, going back to school and getting the grades I needed to get into medical school was a real challenge. But I wanted to be a physician—and I had confidence in myself.

During my first semester at college, I took English composition, biology, algebra, and philosophy. I spent every spare hour studying. But no matter how hard I tried, the best I could get was B's. B's will let many students achieve their goals, but I knew that to get into medical school I had to do better. Other students seemed to put in less time but got better grades; in fact, the same few always got the A's. Were they born with larger brains?

Not willing to give up my goal of becoming a physician—and too proud to admit I might be stupid—I began to look at the students who got the A's. They didn't look exceptionally bright, and they certainly didn't look as if they had stayed up studying all night the way I did. Could they know something I didn't?

I asked them. And through discussions with these A students about their study habits, I began to form a picture of the ingredients of successful study. Skill at note-taking, organization, the use of textbooks and handouts, and good test-taking strategies all seemed to make a real difference. For the most part, the best students all seemed to be doing the same things, so I started trying out their techniques.

My grades improved dramatically that semester, and by the following semester I was receiving straight A's. In fact, I never got another B. Even better, I found it was possible to work *less* and still get better grades! No more sleepless nights, no more frustrating study sessions that ended in a poor grade, no more total panic during exams. With my new study methods in operation, I was able to institute a wonderful rule: no studying after 8 p.m.! Even now, in medical school, I rarely study after 9 p.m.

The year I finished, I was one of three students in Purdue University's School of Science who graduated with highest honors. My 3.96 grade-point average brought offers of three medical school scholarships. This was not the result of my taking a magic potion; it was the result of applying techniques learned from those who got good grades and the decision to focus my energies on achieving that goal.

When my professor asked me to share those techniques with incoming students, I was eager to do so. Memories of my frustrating first semester made me want to help others. But soon after I began to write the how-to paper for incoming freshmen, I realized that the many study methods I used to achieve straight A's would never fit into a six-page essay. That's how this book got started. It grew from a six-page paper into a complete and comprehensive description of my approach toward studying. This book provides you with the means of achieving the grades you want in almost any class under a variety of conditions.

Now let me repeat: You can do it! There is a secret to getting the grades you want in college, and in this book I give you that secret. Not everyone wants to get straight A's, and not everyone needs to; but whatever your goals are, this book will help you attain them. You don't have to be exceptionally intelligent; you don't even have to spend every waking hour studying. But you do have to want to reach your goals, and you have to take all the tips in this book seriously and apply them to your life.

WHO'S GIVING THE ADVICE?

This is a book by students and for students. I'm not the only one who's gotten straight A's using these study methods. In doing the research for this book, I talked with many top students around the country, and their contribution has been invaluable. When I make comments such as, "In my experience . . ." or "It's worked for me," I mean just that; I learned how to get good grades by asking lots of students for their advice and then putting their advice into practice. It worked for me because it had already worked for other students.

If we aren't geniuses, what makes us so smart? Absolutely nothing; this book is not about being smart. We are not more intelligent; we don't even have special memory skills. The primary difference between us and those who work hard but always fall short is this: We have developed a plan of attack, a method of studying that allows us to pack more learning into a shorter period of time. Add to that a willingness to be consistent, to follow the methods, and to devote the time necessary to get the grades—and you'll find that consistently getting A's is not all that difficult.

There are students who are extraordinarily gifted—a very few—but even those with measurably greater IQs don't always earn top grades. The students that contributed to this book are not necessarily brilliant, but they do know how to play the college game.

WHAT'S THE COLLEGE GAME?

A college education is tremendously important for many people; it certainly was for me. While acknowledging its importance, however, I like to think of college as a game. I find it a useful analogy for two reasons:

1. Like most games, you don't have a prayer of winning if you don't know the basic rules; and you probably won't win if you don't develop some advanced strategies. This book gives you both the basic rules and the advanced strategies. It's not just about surviving the college experience—it's about playing and winning the college game. As my instructor pointed out, you'll learn subject matter in your classes, but you won't necessarily learn how to study. That's where this book comes in.
2. College can be a difficult and stressful time. Thinking of college as a game (with admittedly higher stakes than most games) helped me keep it in perspective and reduced my stress level, which made my studying more effective! This whole book is about getting good grades; getting good grades is one of the goals of the college game. But it's not a life-and-death matter. Have you ever heard of people lying on their deathbeds and moaning, "If only I had gotten one more A . . ."? Of course not. Grades are important, but the most important grade you'll ever get in life is the one you give yourself. So think of college as a game. Play it as well as you can, but don't take it too seriously.

WHY, THEN, THE FOCUS ON GRADES?

Maybe you already want good grades and know why. If so, you can skip this section. But for many beginning students, the idea of working for grades conflicts with their ideals about learning for the sake of learning. Don't mistake clear, honest thinking for betrayal of ideals. By understanding the realities of the university system and recognizing that you can move to the top through honest effort, you can serve your own interests without becoming cynical. Suppose you want to become a pediatrician and work in the poorest sections of a big city to help solve poverty-related health problems. That's fine, but you're going to have to get great grades in order to get into a good medical school so that you can get the kind of education that will enable you to help those kids.

Let's take a closer look at what good grades are going to bring you. Those who achieve the highest grades derive personal satisfaction from the realization that all their hard work and effort has paid off. But the accumulation of high grades can pay off in much more than just self-esteem and the knowledge of a job well done. Scholarship money is available for those who achieve high grades—even more than that available for those who excel at sports. Top grades also will bring the attention of graduate and professional schools, which are looking for the best students in the country to attend their programs. If you finish with a top grade-point average, you will have proven yourself a member of that "educational elite," and they will want to know about you.

That same attention will be paid to you by employers if you finish college or graduate school at the top of your class. Those running the largest and most prestigious institutions—law firms, medical research facilities, giant corporations, major newspapers, and so on—all know what it takes to finish at the top, and you will have proven you can do just that. Good grades are the best indication that you know how to work: You know how to organize your life and your time.

HOW CAN READING A BOOK HELP YOU?

"Know-how" is what you're going to get by reading this book. By the end of it, you will *know how* to get the grades you want. You will also *know how* to learn essential material so quickly that you won't have to change your lifestyle—unless you haven't been taking your studies seriously in the least. Once you have mastered the techniques, you will find that you're studying less, receiving better grades, and feeling less stress. But you'll need to take a very practical approach to this book and to your studies. Some points may appear familiar or commonsensical; they are the very points students most often miss.

Are you thinking that it may be hard work, and time-consuming, to read this whole book? You're right. But this is not a book about sidestepping effort. It is about focusing that effort so as to achieve maximum results from your best efforts. There is nothing worse than giving your all and coming up short. Using my methods, your best will translate into top grades.

SUMMARY

☆ I went from being a mediocre high school student to a straight-A college student. If I can do it, so can you. Confidence in yourself and a strong desire to do well are the keys.

☆ This book was written by a student, incorporating suggestions from other students; and it is full of practical advice for doing as well in college as you want to.

☆ Learning the rules of the "college game" and the advanced strategies I provide in this book will equip you to win the game. Thinking of college as a game may help you keep things in perspective and reduce your level of stress.

☆ Good grades can bring you a variety of opportunities that for many people are worth seeking.

☆ Reading this entire book and applying the methods described will allow you to channel your motivation into achievement of the grades you want.

YOU CAN DO IT!

I wouldn't be honest if I didn't tell you that my motivation to become a physician and my confidence in my ability to do so were key factors in my doing well in college. Before you read any further, I'd like you to spend a few minutes thinking about your motivation and your confidence in yourself. Reading the book will be wasted effort if you keep making comments to yourself like "That's too much work for me," "I'll never find time to do that," or "That's beyond my abilities." What you should be saying to yourself instead is "Hey! I could do that—and I'll begin today." Right now, before you read the rest of this book, you need to decide that *you can do it*.

2

You're the Boss on This Job

If you're planning to spend two, four, six, or eight years—and a lot of money—going to college and, maybe, a professional or graduate school, you ought to look at going to school as if it were your job. If going to college is your job, you need to make an important decision. Who is your boss? You could decide to work for the dean of your particular discipline. If that's the case, the professors of individual subjects become the managers in their own departments, and you work for them when you are in that particular area. If you're still living at home, you might decide that your parents, who have been the bosses for quite some time, are still in charge here and that you'll work for them.

But a much better way to look at your education as a job is to make *yourself* the head honcho. I know many of us like to have someone else as the final authority; that way we're not responsible when we goof up. But in this book, *you* are responsible, and you are working for yourself in this company of one. Who else really cares if you do well? Certainly your parents or spouse would be proud if you graduated with honors—or, in some cases, graduated at all—and there may be professors who would be pleased if you did well. But whose career and future is at stake? Only yours.

Probably the best reason for putting yourself in charge of your job as student is the way it makes you approach professors, the dean, and even the president of the college. When you're the boss of your own education, you realize that they work for you! Let's face it: You're certainly paying enough to consider them your employees. This is an important attitudinal distinction, and I think it helps you make the most of your educational experience. You're in charge; others work to help you meet the goals you set for yourself.

Of course, all of this takes place within a university community, which has rules and regulations; and it's your responsibility to follow these. Your enrollment includes an agreement to abide by the school's academic policies and rules of conduct. Your "employees" are similarly bound by specific policies and rules. But that should not make you shift the responsibility for your education from your shoulders to someone else's.

If college is your job, then your earnings are the grades you receive as a result of the work you do. Your company's product is a simple one—your education—and its success is reflected by your grades. Your employees are valuable resources you need to learn how to use effectively and with respect.

WHY ARE YOU GOING TO COLLEGE?

While it may seem premature to discuss your career goals, there is no better time to start formulating some kind of plan for yourself. You're involved in a process that will take anywhere from four to eight years. That's a lot of time, a lot of energy, and a tremendous commitment of your personal resources. Knowing why you are in school will help you stay in school when things get tough—and they will. And it may help you avoid problems that can interfere with your educational goals.

Some students are in school because they have nothing better to do. Others are being pushed by their parents to "get an education." There are people raising their children alone who realize the only way they can earn enough money is by having a degree. There are those who have specific career goals: They may want to become doctors, teachers, veterinarians, lawyers, marine biologists, television announcers, farmers, or business managers. Amidst all these people, there is you. Why are *you* going to college? Answering this question for yourself will be the first building block in your educational career.

Suppose you are one of those students who have no idea "what they want to be when they grow up." College is a good time to decide, at least tentatively. All majors require some general courses in addition to those in the major (if you're a biology major, you'll still need to take classes in the humanities, for example), and you can make use of your first few semesters to take a variety of classes to see what piques your interest. Every college has a career counseling center, where trained counselors can help you explore the variety of job possibilities that await you after college and help you assess your skills, interests, and values. Do some careful thinking about your future. You're much more likely to make the most of college if you're motivated by some long-term goal.

SETTING AND STICKING TO GOALS

While you can't go back and change your past academic record, the future truly does belong to you. When you're the boss, you don't have to get permission from anyone else to make big changes in your life. Even if you were a C or D student one semester, you can become an A student almost overnight—if you're willing to work hard and follow the principles in this book to the letter.

Follow these general guidelines in setting your goals:

◆ Be sure the goal is something you can achieve; be sure you are really setting a tangible goal and not looking toward a vague or distant dream. My long-term goal was to graduate with a B.A. in chemistry, and with highest honors. Yours may be to maintain a solid B average in electrical engineering, or to get A's in all your major classes, or to get grades high enough to earn you a scholarship, or simply to stay off academic probation, or to be the first person in your family to finish college. Whatever your specific long-term goal, this book will give you a good idea about the types of short- and middle-term goals you should be setting to improve your grades.

◆ Be specific in selecting your middle-term goals, and then break them down into achievable units. An application of this break-it-down theory might go something like this: You received a C on the first exam in a particular class, and you wanted an A. Instead of panicking and floundering around, you decide that you are going to shoot for a B on the next test—with the intention of getting A's on the third and following exams. The idea here is to climb, and the speed with which you climb is determined by your motivation and your skills.

◆ Daily, short-term goals are defined by your class requirements. What reading needs to be done? What homework? What work on a term paper? Set these goals high—so high that you almost can't accomplish them. You are your own competition, and you'll only accomplish more by challenging yourself to do more. Making daily goal lists is covered in detail in Chapter 10.

◆ Reward yourself when you have accomplished a goal. You won't find much in the way of a fan club for your efforts at getting good grades, but you can take it upon yourself to acknowledge your own accomplishments.

In many respects, you're like the Greek Sisyphus, condemned to roll a rock up a hill every day only to see it roll back down at night. Every new course taught by a different professor, every research project, every job run by a new boss represents a form of starting over. But the best student has developed the muscles necessary to take him or her to the top over and over again.

The real secret to achieving your goals lies in understanding that many short-term goals add up to middle-term goals, which then naturally grow into long-term achievements. Set some long-term goals, but concentrate on accomplishing the short-term ones today. Get that rock to the top of the hill, and do it again tomorrow.

GRADES, GRADES, GRADES: IS THAT ALL COLLEGE IS?

While grades are the currency of a college education, they are not the entire measure of a successful student—or of a complete person. Other activities—serving in student government, working on a newspaper or literary magazine or for a service or social organization—can contribute both to the time you spend in school and to your future relationships. For some students, part-time work or college sports takes up a great deal of time. When you're trying to decide how much you want to get involved in such activities, it's important to understand the trade-offs involved.

In a management sense (don't forget, you're the boss!), applying a cost-benefit principle to any extracurricular activity will help you make the decision. If you need twelve hours a day to become a top student, and becoming president of the student council means losing three to four hours a day to that pursuit, something has to give. Perhaps the skills you'll gain serving as president will stand you in better stead later in life than getting straight A's—but you're the only one who can guess about that. Volunteer work in a research lab or special-education classroom, participation in a special-interest club, and writing news copy for the campus radio station may be valuable learning experiences and pay off in employment opportunities and graduate school acceptances—or they may eat up so much of your time that you fail your geography class. You're the manager; you decide. It's a good idea to proceed slowly with extracurricular activities until you have a better idea of your abilities as a student. You can always cut back on your activities if you're having a tough time staying afloat in classes.

The same can be said of personal relationships. Many people meet their life partners in college, and my emphasis on straight A's is in no way meant to discourage dating, falling in love, or making friends. But remember your goal. If your relationship with another person supports your goal of getting great grades and finishing at the top of your class, then that should be a strong factor in your attitude about the relationship.

The planning you'll learn to do in this book allows you *more* time for extra activities in your life. For students who don't have a choice about spending time elsewhere—because they work, have a family to care for, or are in college on an athletic scholarship—this book will help you manage your time and teach you how to absorb more in less time.

REMEMBER—IT'S A GAME!

Don't put your entire life—family, friends, entertainment—on hold until the day you've graduated. This is a mistake made by many successful students. They make it to the top of the class but feel miserable and bitter about the sacrifices they made in the pursuit of the letter *A*. While getting excellent grades in college is important and does considerably cut into your free time, it is also important to keep school in perspective with the rest of your life's needs and desires. If you aren't happy with yourself, any success you realize in your college career will be short-lived.

Keep school in perspective. It's important, it's hard work, it takes up the majority of your time when you're doing it—but it isn't your whole life. The methods of study set down in this book can help you avoid the trap of putting your life on hold while you're in college. By organizing your work, setting your goals, and managing your time, you'll have more time and energy available for the rest of your life.

SUMMARY

☆ Look at going to school as a job, and appoint yourself boss.
☆ Think about what you hope to get out of going to college, and use this long-term goal to help you set short- and middle-term goals.

☆ Be aware of the importance of college's "nongraded" activities.

☆ Keep school in perspective. Don't put the rest of your life on hold while you're in college.

YOU CAN DO IT!

Are you ready to take responsibility for being the boss of your work in college? Take a few minutes to think about what you're doing in college. Writing out the answers to the following questions will get you started:

What made you first decide to attend college?

What made you decide to attend this particular school?

How have your ideas about your reasons for attending college changed since your original decision?

What would you like to do when you graduate?

How does that goal fit with your feelings about getting good grades, working hard, and being responsible?

3

Use Not Just Common Sense, But All Your Senses

Do you know why you are more likely to remember TV commercials than lecture information? Because most professors don't dance and sing to help drive the information into your memory. In this chapter, I'll talk about how going to lectures, taking notes, and studying helps you learn—and how you can make the process even more effective by using the techniques outlined in this book.

The stimulus of watching a mugger run down the street with a purse, hearing a person scream, or smelling fire changes our body chemistry. That same kind of change occurs with learning. As information is absorbed or blocked, we continue to be changed chemically; and those chemical changes are the essence of learning. The more senses involved in an experience of learning, the better chance the body has of remembering it; study habits that involve the maximum number of senses are the key to good grades.

Often a teacher who uses props—a tricornered hat when teaching about the Revolutionary War, a skeleton to discuss anatomy—is better at transmitting information to students than one who merely lectures. That's because the teacher makes information come alive for students and allows them to use more than one of their senses. For example, language instructors may have students "act out" words and phrases to help make the information stick. There's nothing like running in place when learning *corriendo* in Spanish class or tipping back a glass of water when it's time to *beber aqua.* It's no coincidence that some of the trivial facts you'll remember for years will be tied to the memory of some funny little bug that landed on the chalkboard. Recently, my neuroanatomy instructor mispronounced a part of the cerebellum called the "flocculus," making it sound like an unmentionable four-letter word. Needless to say, I won't forget that anatomical part come exam time; I'll be able to call it up from memory based on the sight of the word, the sound of a class giggling, and even the feeling of my own laughter.

What does all this have to do with the typical college education? If the instructor and you together are able to involve as many senses as possible in the process of learning, you'll have a much better chance of remembering the material at exam time and later in life. If you review reading materials before a class, this use of your sense of sight lets you form a picture in your brain. During a typical class lecture, your senses of hearing (listening to the lecture) and sight (watching as formulas or ideas are written on the chalkboard) allow you to develop a further understanding of the material. If the class is one that incorporates demonstrations or "hands-on" learning experiences (in labs, for example), your senses of touch, smell, taste, sight, and hearing may all be put to use. Taking notes involves your senses of touch and visualization to reinforce class material and documents the information so it can be studied further at a later date.

The same approach carries over to after-class studying. It has always been difficult for me to commit historical dates or scientific principles to memory; but by using as many senses as possible to "experience" the information, I've been able to do it. Repeating the formula or sentence aloud as I begin to memorize it makes it a sound, and I can use my hearing to help me remember. Writing the information several times on a sheet of scratch paper uses my senses of touch and vision. Later, during a test, if I can't pull up the visual image of the answer, I may be able to remember hearing it or writing it.

I find visualization very important in studying. While I read, I make diagrams, figures, and outlines of the material. The important drawings—those that really seem to help tie the material together—I put in my notes, and every time I review my notes I see them. When I come to these diagrams in my notes, I lean back in my chair, close my eyes, and picture in my mind for a few seconds what that diagram looks like in all its detail. Come exam time, I may have forgotten some obscure point from a lecture that I never dreamed would be on the exam. But I find that if I lean back in my chair, close my eyes, and visualize that list or diagram, it makes it possible to read the obscure point right off my memory.

Others find sound more important, and they may memorize things to the tune of a favorite song. I know someone, for example, who learned to spell "onomatopoeia" by singing it to the tune of the Mickey Mouse fan club song ("M-I-C, K-E-Y, M-O-U-S-E!").

While mathematical equations and lists of French verbs may not be as exciting as an Alfred Hitchcock thriller, the mere act of saying them aloud and then copying them down once or twice helps get the body involved in learning. If you can think of other ways to use more of your senses as you study, it will pay off at test time.

SUMMARY

☆ The more senses involved in a learning experience, the better chance the mind has of remembering it.

☆ Incorporate as many senses as possible into your study routine.

☆ Be aware of the importance of your senses of sight, hearing, and touch as you skim over your textbook reading assignments, attend lectures, take notes, rewrite notes, and chant formulas.

YOU CAN DO IT!

Let's pretend this chapter is something you'll be tested on in a class. How could you use visualization as a technique for remembering the information presented? The main point is that using all your senses enhances learning; the simplest image would probably be a person with ears, eyes, nose, mouth, and hands highlighted.

4

Giving Yourself the Best Shot: Registering for Classes

The best time to begin putting your "I'm-the-boss-on-this-job" attitude to work is at the very beginning, when you register for classes. You may have had some choice about what classes to take in high school, but in college you're the *only person* responsible for fulfilling all the requirements. Your choices of class size, time, instructor, and difficulty can be critical to your grades. And goofing up can have serious long-term consequences—like not being able to graduate with your classmates because you took a freshman literature course instead of a senior one.

KEEP YOUR GOALS IN MIND

We've talked about long-term goals, and this is the first time they come into play. You've got to take courses that will lead to the degree you're interested in earning and do well enough in them to reach your goal. What do you want to do when you graduate? What are you hoping to get from your college education? What should you major in? As a freshman, you may be able to maintain an "undecided" status, and some colleges have General Studies programs in which you don't have to declare a major right away; but the sooner you decide, the less chance there will be of your taking inappropriate courses. It's also possible that as a first-semester freshman you will be "preregistered"—that is, you'll get a schedule in the mail or at orientation. Even if that's the case, you ought to begin thinking about what you need to take and know enough about it to judge whether the courses the computer has signed you up for are appropriate.

READ THE CATALOG

Schools try their best to provide you with the information you need to register for classes. The course catalog is a good place to begin your research, and individual departments also may have materials that spell out what courses are required for various majors. Whatever your major, there are typically

1. a set number of required classes,
2. another group of upper-level classes in your major from which you must select, and
3. a requirement that you take a certain number of liberal arts courses.

After you have fulfilled these obligations, you are free to take "elective" courses. For example, if you're a history major, you'll probably be required to take several lower-level history classes. As you advance through the classes, you probably will be able to choose specialized courses from a set of upper-level history classes. In addition, you'll have to take a certain number of science, math, literature, and other classes, but you'll probably be free to choose those classes from fairly extensive lists. And then there may be some credits you need to earn that can be in any field you're interested in.

The course catalog and department materials should explain all these requirements and provide descriptions of each course that the college offers.

USE YOUR ACADEMIC ADVISER

This is something that different students feel differently about because they've had different experiences. Sometimes your "academic adviser," the faculty member who is supposed to sign your registration forms, is an extremely valuable source of information and guidance. He or she may be able to give you advice about what sorts of nonmajor classes would best help you meet your long-term goals. They may be able to tell you the most useful sequence in which to take these courses. Sometimes they can give you insider information about courses, such as recommending that you take a certain class this year because next year the instructor is going to be in Europe. And if your adviser is someone from whom you also take classes, you may develop a really helpful relationship that can lead to good letters of recommendation, reliable advice about graduate and professional schools, opportunities for independent research or campus employment, and the like.

Unfortunately, it is also possible that your adviser will be someone who is totally uninterested in advising, knows less about course requirements than you do, and serves only as a signature provider. If you're unhappy with your adviser, you can probably change. Select an instructor in your major with whom you'd be comfortable, ask if he or she would be willing to serve as your adviser, and get the forms you need to make the change. Or don't make the change officially—but go to one person for advice and the other for signatures.

If someone gives you advice and it doesn't sound quite right, don't follow it until you've found out for yourself what you ought to do. Don't assume that just because the person giving the advice is someone who *should* know (a student who's taken the class before you, an instructor, an academic adviser) that they actually *do*. I don't mean to give the impression that people out there are intentionally trying to give you bad advice, it's just that no one has as much reason to steer you right as you do yourself. You have to take charge of your own education, and you may as well begin by making yourself the final authority on class requirements.

BALANCE YOUR SEMESTER

One thing to be careful of when you're registering for classes is not to take too many of the same kinds of classes, loading yourself down with too much of the same kind of work and jeopardizing your grades. Most classes can be categorized in a general way as *Mostly Reading, Mostly Writing, Mostly Lecture, Mostly Homework, or Mostly Lab Work*. Each of these types of classes requires a different kind of work (see Chapter 9). Taking a mixture of different kinds of classes will ensure that you're not overloaded with any one type of work. Sometimes the course-catalog description is all you need to determine what the course will require from you; other times, you'll need to talk to other students, your adviser, or the instructor of the course you're considering taking. Ask straightforward questions: Does this class require writing term papers? If so, how many? Does it have independent research project requirements? How many quizzes and exams does this course have? Is field or lab work required?

Study your strengths as well as your weaknesses as a student, and try not to get loaded down with too many of the courses that are hardest for you. For example, if you have math phobia, it would probably be a big mistake to take more than one math class in the same semester. If writing is your big weakness, avoid piling on several Mostly Writing courses during one semester.

And take some fun courses! Taking something you really enjoy can help reduce stress, thus improving your performance in other classes. I don't necessarily mean Basket Weaving 105, although that might be your idea of a fun class. Have you always wanted to play the stock market? Find out if you can take a course that explains investments. Do you love reading novels and short stories? Take American or English literature. Are you interested in plants? Try a general botany course. Don't assume you can't take any upper-level courses outside your major. Sometimes they have prerequisites; but if you're really interested and committed to doing well, a talk with the instructor may be all that's needed to gain admission to the course.

CONSIDER THE TIME THE CLASS MEETS

Try to tailor your schedule to your normal states of alertness. If you feel that you won't be able to discipline yourself sufficiently to get out of bed and to class by 8 a.m., don't sign up for any early classes if you can help it. One of my firmest rules is, *Attend every class!* So if you think you'll be tempted to skip evening classes in order to go to parties or movies, don't sign up for those 7–10 p.m. lectures. If your brain shuts down entirely right after lunch and doesn't begin functioning again until midafternoon, don't register for a lecture course that meets at 1 p.m.: You'll sleep through every lecture. If you're a person who has trouble making use of small blocks of time (an hour or half an hour between classes), try to schedule your classes back to back, leaving yourself large blocks of time for studying.

CLASS SIZE MAKES A DIFFERENCE

Are you going to be able to pay attention to the instructor if the class has 500 students in it? Some students have no problem with big lecture classes, while others feel intimidated or allow themselves to be distracted by all the noise and confusion. You may be able to take the

same class at a different time—perhaps even during a different semester—and have a much smaller set of classmates. Or maybe you
thrive on the large classes; use the same strategy to avoid more inti-
mate classroom settings. If you can't avoid large classes and think you
may have trouble with them, sitting in the front row reduces the distractions and puts you as near the instructor as you might be in a
small class.

SUMMARY

Registering for classes each semester is a critical part of your work.
While academic advisers may help you, ultimately you are the person
responsible for choosing your courses. Remember, taking the right
balance of classes each semester can improve your grades. Here are
my general hints:

☆ Consider your long-term goal when you begin planning your semester schedule.
☆ Use all of the resources—the course catalog, course requirement
  lists, other students, instructors, and your academic adviser—to
  help you decide what you need to take and when you should take
  it.
☆ Consider your interests, your sleep-wake cycle, and your feelings
  about class size when you plan your schedule.
☆ Try to avoid loading yourself down with too many classes from any
  one category (Mostly Lecture, Mostly Lab Work, Mostly Reading,
  Mostly Writing, Mostly Homework) when you plan your semester
  schedule.

YOU CAN DO IT!

When you're thinking about what classes to take each semester, you need to consider the variety of factors that I cover in this chapter. Assessing your own personality, goals, and preferences is an important first step. To help get you started, read the following statements and place a check mark next to those that describe you. Then think about how the statements you checked will influence your performance in college.

I know exactly what I want to get out of being in college.

I am more interested in getting a general education than in earning a specific degree.

I am planning to take a wide variety of classes before I make any decisions about my major.

I have declared a major and don't expect to change.

I like to get up bright and early and get right to work.

My brain doesn't really function until sometime after lunch.

With discipline, I could force myself to get to early classes on time.

Writing has always been easy for me.

Writing has always been a chore for me.

Math classes have always been easy for me.

Math classes have always been a chore for me.

Reading has always been easy for me.

Reading has always been a chore for me.

As you consider what courses to take next semester, use this matrix to help you avoid taking too many classes requiring the same types of work. List the course titles in the column on the left, and place a check mark under the heading that most accurately describes each one. Use information from the course catalog, instructors, and other students to categorize each course. If you end up with too many courses in any one category, consider another combination of courses.

Course Title	Mostly Lecture	Mostly Writing	Mostly Reading	Mostly Lab Work	Mostly Homework
1.					
2.					
3.					
4.					
5.					
6.					
7.					
8.					

Chapter

5

The Instructor Is Your Most Valuable Resource

I've stressed before that the only person you really can depend on is yourself. But your number one resource in the pursuit of top grades will be the instructor. Remember, as the boss of your education, you *employ* instructors to work for you, and you need to learn to use this resource effectively and with respect to help you get good grades.

FIND OUT ABOUT INSTRUCTORS BEFORE YOU SIGN UP FOR CLASSES

The person teaching your class can make a tremendous difference both in how much you learn and in the grade you receive, and the time to research instructors is *before* signing up for courses. Seek out students who have already taken courses from the instructors you're considering for the following semester. Ask what you can expect in the form of tests, grades, and the instructor's ability to teach the material. Success in later years in college and graduate school is dependent on hard knowledge, so getting the "easy" instructor in a key course or subject is not always the smart way to go. On the other hand, purposefully taking a course from a professor who is notorious for handing out low grades may not be good for your grade-point average. Keep in mind who the information is coming from, though—with the study habits you'll learn in this book, you may well get an A from that "impossible" instructor.

Going through the grapevine is not the only way to find out about instructors. Here are others:

◆ Student government offices and sororities and fraternities sometimes keep files of information about various courses and instructors.

◆ Most colleges give awards to instructors for exceptional teaching, and a list of such award winners should be available, perhaps from the student newspaper or college public relations offices.

◆ Student evaluations of courses and instructors are sought and made public by some schools, giving you access to a summary of student opinions instead of just the advice of a few.

◆ Instructors whose advice you trust may be able to recommend others whose classes you would enjoy or do well in.

At some universities you'll have the opportunity to take classes with people who know more about their subject than anyone else in the country—or even the world. Seize these opportunities! If your interest is nuclear physics, don't pass up the chance to take a class with, or even hear a single lecture by, a Nobel Prize winner in this field. If your interest *isn't* nuclear physics, perhaps it would be if you were exposed to a leader in the field. Take advantage of the opportunities you'll have to come in contact with great minds.

Another factor to consider is the long-term plans of your instructors. Are they going on sabbatical next year when you were planning on taking their course? There is nothing more frustrating than finally figuring out the exact sequence of courses you need to take in your major and then having to junk the whole plan because the first instructor you hoped to have is heading for Egypt next semester.

INTRODUCE YOURSELF EARLY IN THE SEMESTER

Most instructors care about students and are there to help them learn. They'll be even more interested in doing that if you make it clear you're there to do the learning. In a small class, it's possible that your class attendance, performance, and participation will speak for itself. But in the many large classes you'll encounter, you'll be nothing but a student ID number on a computer printout unless you make a special effort to get to know your instructor. I recommend that you introduce yourself to the instructors in all your classes, large or small, during the first week of the semester. The instructor's concern for you is going to be considerably less if the first time you show up in the office is the day before an exam instead of early in the semester.

How should you introduce yourself? Go to the instructor's office during office hours. Let them know who you are and what your intentions are regarding their courses. Talk to them about how it fits into your long-range plans. If you're a science major taking an English composition course, let the teacher know that and explain why you want to do well. If you're a philosophy major taking introductory chemistry, tell the instructor what you're doing in the class. Don't waste the instructor's time: Just introduce yourself briefly. Note also that while you want to let the instructor know that you want and plan to do well—that is, to get a good grade—you *don't* want to say, "I need to get an A."* Instructors will be more receptive to someone who seems interested in learning than to someone who seems only to want to get a good grade.

Still have cold feet? Okay. I'll give you a sample of what you should say. Let's say the class is English composition. Knock on the instructor's door during office hours, stick your head in, and say, "Hi, Dr. So and So. My name is John Stowers. Do you have a minute to talk?" Then get your whole body into the office, sit down, and say, "I just wanted to introduce myself and let you know that I'm a premed student. It's important that I do well in this class. I'm not much good at writing, but I know it's really important to be able to write well, and since I'm thinking of going into medical research I know I'll need to be able to put together good research reports. I'm a hard worker and would appreciate any suggestions you can give me." Then let the instructor talk, and then get out.

Now maybe the instructor will be impressed, or maybe he or she will be shocked. This may be the first time they've ever had a student introduce himself. Or maybe they're thinking, "Gee, I wish this jerk would get out of here. I have work to do." Those are the chances you take. But if they see you making an effort in class, they'll forget what they thought before—and just remember *you*.

INSTRUCTORS DO MORE THAN LECTURE

When you have trouble in understanding class material, get help from the instructor. Instructors have weekly office hours set aside for stu-

---

*If you are on the border between an A and a B at the end of the semester, it may help if you tell the instructor honestly that you need an A—and why.

dents who require additional help.* Seeking this help doesn't mean you're not a good student; on the contrary, asking questions shows instructors that you've been paying attention in class and thinking about what's been presented. So don't hesitate to take advantage of the additional help instructors can provide. Because few people take advantage of office hours, they can often turn into one-on-one tutorial sessions for you, enabling you to master the course material like no one else in your class.

It's important to be well-prepared with your questions when you approach an instructor. They want to help you—but they don't want to waste time. Don't expect them to help if you haven't done your share. If readings or homework problems have been assigned, tackle them *before* you seek extra assistance. Then follow these steps:

1. Have questions written out so you won't forget what you came for.
2. Bring your class notes along if your question relates to them, or your textbook or handouts if they are relevant.
3. Be ready to show the instructor how you've already attempted to solve the problem.
4. Ask your question, then listen carefully to the instructor's explanation and take notes to help you remember.
5. If you're not sure you understand what you're being told, thank the instructor, tell him or her that you'll go over the material (or try the problem) again, and ask if you may return for further help if you're still confused.
6. If you *know* you don't understand and feel that the instructor has already done everything possible to explain, ask for recommendations for other sources of help.

The time spent in the office with your instructor is important for many reasons. First, it helps you understand the material better. Second, it shows your instructor that you are making an effort to learn the material and are concerned about doing well in class. Third, problems you may have in understanding lecture material are often the same problems other students are having, and pursuing these helps the instructor recognize questions the whole class may be having.

Fourth, and often most important, making good use of instructors'

---

*Some part-time or adjunct faculty may not have office hours (or even offices), and some faculty who set office hours may not keep them. Sometimes scheduled office hours will conflict with your class or work schedule. When you need to meet with an instructor, don't let nonexistent or inconvenient office hours stop you. Make an appointment, and then follow my tips for using that time effectively.

office hours can pay off at exam time if you ask the right questions and pay particular attention to the *way* your instructor answers them. For example, if you ask a simple question about a point in the lecture and your instructor gives you a simple answer, without much attention to whether you really understood it, this is probably a sign that it's not a very important point—and that it probably won't be a significant part of the next exam. On the other hand, if your simple question is answered in great detail and with obvious concern for your understanding, it's very likely that it *will* be on the next exam. Often to get full credit on exam questions, key words or points must be used. Take note of these when your questions are being answered by your instructor.

In many large universities, lower-division undergraduate courses have teacher aides (graduate students) who teach anywhere from 200 to 400 students or serve as assistants in proctoring exams and grading homework assignments. The professor may not be available for help, but the aide is. Don't be alarmed. Students who have reached the graduate level in a discipline and are offered this kind of position are usually very knowledgeable—and often far more eager to help than is the professor. They also may be in charge of grading exams and homework papers and can influence your final grade in the same ways that the "real" instructor can.

Many instructors offer occasional extra study sessions or regular recitation classes for discussing homework problems. *Don't miss these!* If instructors are willing to spend extra time helping you, you'd better show up for help. As in discussions during office hours, these review sessions can give you a good idea what questions will be on the exam and how to answer them. And other students' questions may provide clues you'd never think of on your own.

THE SYLLABUS IS A CONTRACT WITH THE INSTRUCTOR

Most teachers will provide a syllabus and a brief outline of the course, including specific details about exam dates, quizzes, and what components of the course will be used to determine your grade. This is, in effect, a contract for performance. In exchange for certain work in the class, you receive a final grade.

Make sure at the beginning of the semester that there are no hidden agendas, no blind corners, no misunderstandings regarding this contract between you and the instructor. Go over the syllabus carefully, and be sure you understand what's expected of you. Quizzes, homework, term papers, lab reports, and tests should all carry specific weights in the final grade. Class participation or attendance may be considered in your final grade; be sure you have that defined. What constitutes "good" class participation? What should you do if you must miss a class? If there are any uncertainties about any part of the syllabus, discuss them with the instructor at the beginning of the semester. While the teacher may grade you occasionally throughout the semester, you should keep track of your progress almost weekly (if not class by class; see Chapter 11), and you can't do that if you don't know what your grade depends on.

PERCEPTION IS EVERYTHING—OR AT LEAST A GREAT DEAL

The rapport you establish with your instructors can be critical to your grade. The teacher's view of you as a student is crucial. If you are *perceived* as a great student, many minor mistakes may be overlooked because the instructor will be looking for your successes. This is just human nature at work. If you are seen as a marginal student, then every mistake, major or minor, sticks in their minds and helps to lower any grade they may be considering for your work. This may not be fair, but it is the nature of the game. The impression you make will help elevate you to the top of the class or depress your grade to the point that you may never break away from the pack.

I can't emphasize this point enough. Many instructors I have spoken with admit that the educational process is more subjective than anyone likes to admit. Your instructor's perception of you as a student will unavoidably influence your grade. If you project the image of a great student, they will treat you like a winner; and often this will reflect itself in higher marks. You can get this process off to a good start by introducing yourself at the beginning of the semester and letting the instructor know you'll be taking their class very seriously. Then follow it up by *being* a great student.

SEE THE INSTRUCTOR AS A PERSON

Your relationship with your instructors is a key factor in getting good grades. It helps you make the most of your education if you think of yourself as the boss, but you also need to have a genuine respect for your instructors' knowledge and for their profession. Don't make the mistake of thinking the person before you is "just a teacher." Often students fail to realize that their instructors may have given up more lucrative careers because they recognized and wanted the personal rewards that teaching offers. Indeed, the majority of teachers care about their students and are there to help them learn. Also, most instructors care, some passionately, about their subjects. They may be engaged in research in some specialty in their field, and if you show an interest in what they've dedicated their lives to, they're much more likely to want to talk to you—and to remember you favorably.

DON'T BE A TEACHER'S PET

Some of the advice I've given may sound as if all you have to do is become a teacher's pet and your A is assured. While I do think it's important to take advantage of opportunities to learn more from the instructor, you'll be getting yourself into real trouble if you come across as just full of hot air. In fact, you should use office hours only to ask questions—not to propound your latest theory of relativity. Instructors know the difference between someone trying to show off and someone trying to do well in class through honest effort. Showing off wastes your time and the instructor's time, and it rarely does your grade any good.

INSTRUCTORS GIVE MORE THAN GRADES

Your relationship with the instructor helps to create the framework for a good letter of recommendation from him or her when you apply to a graduate school or for a job. Of course, to obtain good letters of recommendation from instructors, you first have to achieve good grades and give the instructor something positive to comment on. Good letters are particularly important to students who plan to pursue graduate degrees because most programs require letters of recommendation from undergraduate instructors. They also come in handy for job applications, however. On many job applications, you have to list references, and a good relationship with your instructors paves the way to having them agree to serve as a reference for you. Start looking for instructors you feel might write a good letter in support of your application to advance in their field of study. Once you find such instructors, get to know them and plan on doing exceptionally well in their classes.

It's a good idea to contact instructors while your class performance is still fresh in their minds. Ask them if they would be willing, when needed, to write a letter of recommendation or serve as a reference for you. Some people like to write the letter while they still remember you clearly and then keep it in a file until it's needed, which is another good reason to ask right after you've taken their class. Most instructors are more than willing to write letters for good students, so don't hesitate to ask.

SUMMARY

Your instructors are your most valuable resource during your entire college career. I recommend the following to be sure you don't waste this resource:

☆ Research the instructors before signing up for classes. Sources of information include other students, other instructors, student government and sororities and fraternities, lists of "outstanding teacher" award winners, and written student evaluations.

☆ Introduce yourself to your instructors early in the semester. Let them know why you're taking their class and that you want and plan to do well.

☆ Use office hours and extra study sessions to get help with homework assignments and to have questions from lectures or your readings answered. Follow my tips for preparing for such sessions.

☆ Realize that it's your responsibility to be sure you understand and meet the requirements of the instructor's contract for an A.

YOU CAN DO IT!

Do you know your instructors, or do you feel like a face in the crowd? If you feel uncertain about following my advice for introducing yourself to your instructors, do it by using their office hours to get help. Find something you need extra information about, and follow my tips on page 25. But before you launch into your questions, say, "My name is John Stowers, and I'm in your Sociology 101 class that meets at 11 in Hanser Hall. Could I ask you a couple of questions?" Nothing profound—but at least you've taken the first step.

6

Classmates Provide Competition and Companionship

Classmates help to determine the level you'll have to reach to have the highest grades in the class. But you don't have to see that from a negative viewpoint; in fact, other good students are great for motivation. If you know they're studying hard and getting good grades, it motivates you to work harder.

MAKE FRIENDS WITH ANOTHER GOOD STUDENT

My most memorable college year was my sophomore year, when I met Paul Coelho, one of the contributors to this book. By our sophomore year, Paul and I were A students and had the same goal of going to medical school. After our first exam in the class in which we met, I knew that he was my only competition for the highest grade in the class. We both have competitive natures, and this added a whole new dimension to this class and all the others we took together.

Shortly after that first exam, we made a wager that whoever got the highest score on the next exam would be treated to lunch by the other. I don't remember who won this first bet (of course, if you asked Paul he would tell you he was the winner), but the final score doesn't matter. What really matters is that these friendly wagers made the class more interesting and inspired us to study harder. In the end the lunches came out about even, despite the multitude of bets over two years. Fortunately for our friendship, our graduating grade-point averages were nearly identical. We had both started at the bottom of our class and graduated at the top.

I highly recommend forming this kind of close association with someone taking classes in your area of study, someone who, like you, is striving to be the best in the class. Seek out a serious acquaintance, *not* someone hoping you'll pull them through. Look for students who have the kinds of qualities you are hoping to develop in yourself. Other good students will challenge you to achieve more.

While friendly competition can be beneficial to your grade and provide you with some laughs, it is important to remember to keep it friendly. See this person as your partner. If your competitor does better, it will inspire you to do better. Work as a team. When Paul and I were betting lunches on test scores, I often asked him how much he studied over a weekend; and I used this as a gauge for my own efforts. I assume he did the same. Our friendly competition made school more fun, and we could always count on each other for help when faced with difficult material.

THE DOWN SIDE OF COMPETITION

Unfortunately, the competition provided by classmates in general can have a less beneficial effect. The curve system in its most medieval form pits classmates against one another: The better they do, the worse *you* do—in terms of grades. On the other hand, the people earning C's help others earn A's. Without all the students doing mediocre or poor work in college, there would *be* no straight-A students. Someone has to get the B's, the C's, the D's, and the F's. Others therefore will be hoping you're going to do poorly, and occasionally others may even *help* you do poorly. Tactics such as stealing class notes, ruining lab experiments, and cheating on exams are not unknown in the college environment. Look out for competing classmates who stoop to such tactics, and don't be drawn into it yourself. Cheating may buy you time, but in the long run it will lead to failure.

From the other perspective, you may not be comfortable thinking of your classmates as the people who will help you do well by doing poorly themselves. You're not going to *make* them do poorly; it's just one of the unfortunate realities of the curve system of grading that some students get lower grades than others. Not everyone can be at the top of the class.

I think that it pays to be friendly and helpful to your classmates. What goes around comes around, and I think it's best to help classmates who ask for help. You may be in a position to need help from someone yourself someday, and helping another student is not going to jeopardize your grade.

Let me temper that advice with this caution: It's not your job to become a teacher or to spend all your time listening to others complain about how difficult the class is. It may be that there are a few people you enjoy working with; keep it to that number. Often teaching someone else will help you tighten your grasp of the information, but don't spend all your time teaching. Getting straight A's in college is very time-consuming, and taking on the work of teacher can severely distract from your own studies.

CLASSMATES PROVIDE HELP IN MANY WAYS

There are other practical benefits to be derived from being on friendly terms with your classmates. When you miss a class due to illness or another serious problem, you can use your friendly relationship with other students to get a decent set of notes to copy. Or there may come a time when you reach a snag and just can't assimilate a concept; check with one of your classmates.

Regularly reviewing class materials with a group of students may help you study more effectively. Some colleges feel study groups are so effective that students are assigned to such groups before classes begin, and others provide assistance in forming study groups. If your school hasn't institutionalized this procedure, you may want to form your own study group. Choose a few students you think you would feel comfortable working with, and plan to meet regularly to go over notes and clarify lecture material. Some study groups meet weekly; others meet after every class. Special sessions are often scheduled to prepare for exams. One way to conduct such a group is for one member to "redeliver" the lecture while the others make additional notes, ask questions, and comment when they feel the "lecturer" misunderstood a point.

Once you've developed a few relationships with serious and dependable students, you can begin using that network for other purposes. For example, exams given previously by particular instructors can help track their thinking and thus help you in the test you're about to take. Put the word out through your network that you want to find those old exams. You don't have to be Lewis and Clark searching out new territory for each class. Someone almost always has gone before you; in almost every class I have ever taken, at least a few students have obtained old exams from friends who have already taken the class. In most cases they'll give copies to you, particularly if you have been generous with them.

Finding a student who has taken a class before you can also give you insight into what needs to be done to get an A, and this is easier to accomplish when you have established a network of friendly and serious classmates. Ask around until you find someone who knows someone who has taken the class. Then seek that person out and talk over the importance of homework assignments, textbook reading, and other course components.

Being on friendly terms with other serious students is a big plus in classes where you need a lab partner or one or more group-project partners. These group projects can be tough anyway, but I can't imagine anything worse than working on a paper with students who have no interest in doing a good job. The best possible outcome would be to do all the work yourself to be sure it's done well, but it's not a pleasant experience. When you know a few good students, you can choose to work with them on such projects.

Classmates are a great "nonofficial" source of information, too; and sometimes that information saves you time and trouble. Maybe someone knows that you ought to take Dr. Smith's class before Dr. Black's, even though they're not really "sequential courses," and that you then shouldn't let too much time elapse before you take your Graduate Record Exams because the two courses together are so helpful. And someone else has heard that even though the syllabus says you have to know the chief exports of every country, what Dr. Simmons actually is interested in is the southern hemisphere. Of course, sometimes such information is unreliable; but typically it's useful enough so that students who are "out of the loop"—part-time or night students, for example—can be at a real disadvantage. If you are one of these "disadvantaged" students, it's worth making an extra effort to get into the network (see Chapter 14).

HOW DO YOU MEET GOOD STUDENTS?

I've tried to convince you to make friends with other students who are aiming for the top. How do you find these helpful classmates? There are a number of possible approaches.

1. You can keep your eye on your fellow classmates. Who is doing particularly well? Who seems to grasp concepts quickly and speaks up in class with confidence and ease?
2. You can pay attention during class discussions to the students who

have interesting questions or comments and catch up with them after class to continue the discussion.

3. You can keep an eye out for students who seem to be paying attention during lecture and who are obviously engaged in taking notes (versus gazing out the window, for example).

4. Clubs and activities related to your area of study are excellent sources for meeting serious students. Join the entomology club if you're in biology or the theater group if you're in speech and communications. Sometimes such activities end up taking too much of your time, but there's no reason you can't drop out later if that turns out to be the case—and by that time you will have made some friends.

SUMMARY

Although classmates compete with you for top grades, a friendly relationship with at least one other student can do a lot for your motivation. Remember these tips:

☆ Classmates can help you with difficult concepts and serve as important sources of lecture notes, old exams, and nonofficial information about classes and instructors. Participating in study groups may help you study more effectively.

☆ Avoid students who are just looking for a free tutor or someone with whom to complain about the unfairness of life. Don't sink with their ship.

☆ Associate with students who challenge you to reach higher.

YOU CAN DO IT!

Take a few minutes to think about your college friends (or high school friends if you're just starting college). Do they contribute to your studying effectively, or do they distract you? Do they challenge you to do better, or do they lean on you too heavily for help? Do they support your goals, or do they ridicule them? Are you content with your friends, or do you think you might do better to find some new ones? Associating with the right people in college can make a big difference in your struggle to improve your performance.

7

Let's Go to Class

Sure, you have to study to get straight A's. But there's something more fundamental: *You've got to go to class.* And before you go, you need to be prepared. While you're there, you've got to pay attention, participate, and take excellent notes. When class is over, you have to rewrite those notes and be sure you understand everything that was covered in class. In this chapter, I'll tell you how to prepare, provide tips for class participation, and describe note-taking and note-rewriting procedures.

Following this one simple rule—go to class—will give you a big advantage over the many students who look at lectures as something to be avoided whenever possible. And knowing what to do in class and what to do right after class will boost you above the students who attend lectures but don't pay much attention or take decent notes. You're well on your way to straight A's, and you haven't even started to study.

BEGIN BEFORE THE BEGINNING

I find it helpful to go to school the day before classes begin, look up the room numbers, and get to know my way around campus. There's nothing worse than walking in late on your first day of class and having everyone stare at you.

But I recommend preparing for your first classes earlier than that day-before campus tour. Whenever you can, get all your books for all your classes at least a week in advance. Take some time to familiarize yourself with the course content. If you know what material will be covered in the first week of class, read it before class begins. If you can't find out from the instructor or from students who have taken the course recently, simply read the first chapter of each textbook. Occasionally you may buy the wrong book or read the wrong material because there has been a last-minute faculty reassignment or some other problem. But I believe the hassle of occasionally having to return a book is far outweighed by the benefit of having your books early.

Buying your books early has a couple of advantages. First, and most practically, you won't have to stand in those unbelievably long lines in the bookstore during the first week of classes, and you won't risk the book being sold out before you get there. Second, you'll be prepared to begin absorbing lecture material right away, while others are casting around for a reference point. Instead of floundering around, you'll feel ahead of the game right from the start; and that's an important psychological advantage.

You should be preparing for exams, midterms, and finals from the first day of classes, and getting your books early allows you to start even before classes begin. If it's not possible to get your books before classes begin, at least get them as soon as possible, and do that first week's worth of reading immediately. This early work will help you do well on the first-semester exam—the one most people do worst on. Nailing this first exam makes you look like one of the smart ones in the class, gives you confidence, and challenges you to do even better on the next exam.

PREVIEW COURSE MATERIAL REGULARLY

It's helpful to get a jump start on classes, and you can continue to be ahead of the game by using my system of previewing course material. Never go to a lecture unprepared. Before attending any lecture, skim through any assigned (or unassigned but pertinent) section of reading on the topic to be covered. During this skim, pay particular attention to the pictures, diagrams, graphs, and subheadings. While I'm reading, I make diagrams in the margins of my book or syllabus and try to sketch out the order of events or the points in a theory. Use your sense of sight to get an overview of the general direction of the class lecture and its basic content. This prepares your brain by creating a visual context that can be filled in with the audio during lecture.

As the class lectures become more detailed, you'll need to be able to order those details quickly and effectively in your brain. Your brain is not unlike a warehouse, where putting something away is only half the battle; being able to find it again is the real victory. Previewing the lecture material by reading class handouts or the assigned sections of the text makes it possible for me to put away facts more quickly and effectively during a lecture.

THE LECTURE: BE THERE BEFORE IT EVEN STARTS

Instructors normally cover the most important information during the class lecture; this material may represent 80 to 90 percent of the exam material. My hard-and-fast rule is worth repeating: *Always attend class!* Never miss. This is one of the easiest things you can do to get yourself in position to be a straight-A student.

Why is it so important to go to every class? In some classes, much of what the instructor says in the lecture is also in the textbook. But most instructors will provide *more* information than is available in the text. And during the lecture, the instructor explains the material and brings it to life with examples, demonstrations, jokes, stories, recent research findings, slides, overheads, movies, and even guest speakers. The instructor's choice of what to cover in the lecture lets you know what is important and significant—and what you'd better study if you want to do well on the exam. If you aren't there, you'll never know.

Why do I say to be there before the lecture begins? If you dash in at the last moment, you'll be unpacking your backpack or trying to find the right notebook while the instructor is beginning to introduce the day's topic, or reviewing important points from the last lecture, or discussing the main points for the upcoming exam—and you won't hear it. To make the most of each lecture, you need to be in your seat, notebook out and open, pen ready, and listening *before* the instructor begins. Better yet, you should have enough time to spend a minute glancing at the notes from the last lecture to see if you had any questions you needed to ask or simply to remind yourself what was being discussed when the last class ended.

A serious student should try to sit as close to the front of the class as possible, and this is another good reason for getting to class before it begins. Brownie points? Not really. The first reason is simply to hear better, whether you're using your ears alone or a tape-recorder microphone to record the lecture. Especially in large lecture halls, you may miss some of the lecture because of any number of extraneous noises: rustling papers, other students giggling and talking, heating vents blowing. If you are taping the lecture, you will have a better chance of picking up the instructor's voice from the front row. The second reason is that sitting up front helps you to stay focused on the material being presented. Even if you can hear perfectly from the back row, you'll have fewer distractions if you sit closer to the front. The fewer people between you and the instructor, the more likely you are to pay attention for the whole lecture.

BE MORE THAN A WARM BODY

Just being in class is not enough. You have to be a prepared and active participant. How often have we been told that "there's no such thing as a stupid question"? Go ahead and ask your questions, whether you think they're stupid or not. Clarify any uncertainties you have right when you have them. If you don't get your question answered during class, ask it again after class; or try to get help from the textbook. Make sure your notes reflect the confusion at hand so you don't forget to get it resolved.

Most instructors welcome questions and comments. Imagine how boring it must be to recite the same material over and over, particularly to a room full of zombie-type students. Students who pay attention and think about the material being presented are a welcome change from these night-of-the-living-dead types. Sure, some professors are boring; but if you pay attention to the presentation and really work to understand it, you may be surprised at how even the driest lecturers begin to seem more human—and more interesting.

Asking questions can help the instructor gauge the effectiveness of the presentation, too. If you're one of the best students in class and you have a question that needs clarification, how confused is the worst student in class? Do yourself and your classmates a favor by bringing up questions.

But don't just raise your hand when you don't know or understand something; engage the instructor and bring forward your own reaction to the topic at hand. As you become more engaged with the instructor, an interesting phenomenon will occur—he or she will begin to focus more closely on your section of the class during the lectures. This focused attention can make the class more interesting for you;

the lecture becomes more of an interactive, learning conversation than a one-way lecture. Some of the most interesting and informative classes I've taken were the ones in which the instructor encouraged class participation. One caution: Don't go to extremes. Neither the instructor nor the rest of the class will appreciate your efforts if you take up most of every class with your contributions and questions.

TAKE THE WORLD'S BEST NOTES

Ever heard the expression "straight from the horse's mouth"? Racetrack touts use the expression to describe the validity of their information. In the classroom, the same principle applies. But here, the horse is the instructor. What the instructor says during lectures is as important as knowing which horse ate its Wheaties this morning.

For most classes, the most important study resource you have available is your own set of lecture notes. The notes you take during a lecture are your record of what the professor said; the better your notes, the better the record. Some instructors may lean heavily on the textbook for exam material, but it is my experience that information from lectures is a very important part of any examination. Instructors tend to lecture from a set of their own notes, and they use those notes to make up exam questions. The better your notes are, the more closely they will resemble the instructor's notes—and the more prepared you'll be for exam questions.

Taking the Notes

When I say take complete notes, I mean *complete*. Don't just jot down a few key words or the things the instructor writes on the board. Try to write down everything the instructor says that is relevant to the material being covered. Make up a system of shorthand if you have to, or rely on a tape recorder—but be sure your notes are complete.

Here are some specific hints for good note taking:

◆ Make up and use abbreviations or symbols for words or phrases that are going to be used frequently in the lecture; e.g., "E. H." for Ernest Hemingway, "phot" for photosynthesis, "GNP" for gross national product. Use arrows, equal signs, and other symbols to indicate relationships.

◆ If you miss something, indicate it in your notes with a large question mark so that you can fill in the missing information later with the help of classmates, the textbook, or the instructor.

◆ Pay attention to the emphasis the instructor places on various topics, and underline or star particularly important points. Often instructors tell you quite clearly what they consider to be important—and what will be on the exam—by saying things such as, "The *key to understanding* Plato's argument is . . ." or "The *single most critical* stage in the depression/recession cycle is. . . ."

◆ If the instructor uses slides or overheads and you don't have time to get what you need from them, ask after class if you can see them again to copy important information. Your request may not be granted, but it doesn't hurt to try.

The key to good note taking is paying attention. You have to be listening—not snoring, not doodling, not passing notes, not doing your homework, not writing a letter, but *listening*—and writing it all down.

If the speed of the instructor's lecture or your note-taking ability prevents you from taking complete notes, tape-record the lecture or arrange with other students to compare notes. The ability to improve your notes after a lecture is one of the benefits of working with a study group (see sample of notes on pages 45–46).

Rewriting Lecture Notes

Rewrite your lecture notes after every class. Some top students say they never do this. But I have found that listening and taking notes requires so much energy and attention that it's difficult to comprehend the material being presented. My strategy is to take legible, comprehensive notes; any points that elude me during the lecture I pick up that evening when I rewrite and review my notes. If you find that you can take good notes and still understand the whole lecture and that rewriting notes doesn't help you, don't waste time doing it. Some students prefer simply to read over their notes and fill in the holes without completely rewriting. But I have never found it to be a waste of time.

The rewriting process should not be simply a matter of copying; rather, you should be reorganizing the notes, putting pieces together, creating order out of chaos. If the instructor began explaining the causes of World War II and then went off on a tangent about Hitler, your notes can be rewritten so that the causes are all listed in one neat section. If you got confused during a description of waste management procedures, you can look it up in the textbook or ask other students for help and fill in the gaps. This is the time to be sure you understand what the lecture was all about. Is there something that doesn't quite fit, that still doesn't make sense? Keep a list of questions to ask, either at the beginning of the next lecture or during your instructor's office hours.

By making it a point to rewrite class notes after every lecture, you can concentrate on taking accurate and complete notes in class without worrying. You know that you'll be able to organize the information later. Rewriting is also a very effective way to absorb more information from the lecture notes, making the procedure a useful study tool. And by rewriting your notes, you provide yourself with a clear, easy-to-read set of notes for reviewing and studying the rest of the semester (see sample of notes on pages 45–49).

Taping Lectures

If you tape lectures, be sure you mark the tapes well and keep an orderly tape library. If you have no intention of doing so, you may as well not keep the tapes because finding particular lectures will be impossible once you lose track. If you do tape lectures, you can put those tapes to good use on long drives or while working on your tan out by the pool. And, of course, you can use them to fill in the holes in your written notes.

I always felt that if I taped lectures, I'd be tempted to drift off to sleep in class; others find it extremely useful and say that taping allows them to really listen and try to understand the material during class instead of frantically trying to write everything down. You'll have to decide what works best for you. If you do tape lectures, I recommend writing out your notes from the tape as soon as possible after each lecture, which means you'll be listening to the lecture twice in one day.

Making Up Condensed Notes

Another very important learning technique is to make up a set of abbreviated notes. This works particularly well for classes such as chemistry, physics, biology, geology, and history—classes where large amounts of new material are presented on a daily basis. To make up a condensed set of notes, take the time each day after rewriting to comb through your lecture notes for definitions, formulas, and theories, and place them on a sheet of paper in a very brief and condensed form. These notes should be so condensed that several days of notes will fit on a single sheet of paper. (Be careful not to condense them so much that you have to use a magnifying glass to read them.) Only the most important materials, in an abbreviated form, should be included.

While these notes are no substitute for your original class notes, they are an excellent way of committing many facts to memory. Because they are so condensed, they can be carried in a shirt pocket or purse and pulled out and reviewed several times a day. Condensed notes allow you to make better use of odd bits of spare time throughout the day: driving to school or work, eating lunch, or waiting for class to begin (see sample on page 49).

Using Flash Cards

Flash cards—pieces of paper with one bit of information on the front and some corresponding information on the back—can be a useful tool if you want to memorize and organize large amounts of material. The types of information for which they are particularly helpful include species names, vocabulary words, molecular structures and names, and key events and dates in history. Because each bit of information is on its own card, you can organize all of it in a variety of ways, increasing the chances of your remembering bits and pieces at test time. For example, you could organize a set of flash cards on British rulers alphabetically, chronologically, according to politics, by length of life, or with respect to allies. Each time you reorganize them, you are forced to look at the information in a new way.

Flash cards should be kept simple, and they should not substitute for reviewing lecture notes and class material for exams. Sometimes the hours spent producing flash cards could be used more effectively to review notes. To determine how simple flash cards should be, try to gauge the amount of time it takes to make them and the percentage of the test that you expect them to help with. If all your study time is spent making flash cards of bird species and their habitats and two-thirds of the exam is on migration patterns and mating behavior, then your flash cards are not simple enough. As is the case with rewriting notes and taping lectures, some students swear by flash cards while others find them of little use. Try it, and then decide for yourself.

SUMMARY

It may seem as if I've presented a lot of information here. But my advice boils down to this:

☆ Get your textbooks a week ahead of time so that you can preview the first week of lecture material.

☆ Go to campus the day before classes begin and locate all your classrooms.

☆ Never miss a class, get there early, and sit at the front of the room.

☆ Preview lecture material by reading class handouts and skimming the textbook assignments for three classes ahead of time.

☆ Ask questions, and be an active participant in class.

☆ Take complete notes without worrying too much about understanding every detail of the lecture. Concentrate on getting everything down on paper.

☆ Rewrite your notes, filling in the gaps by talking to other students or finding information in the textbook. Then reorder the notes logically.

☆ Make a set of condensed notes after every class by pulling key concepts, terms, tables, or graphs from your class notes.

Now that you know what to do before, during, and after classes, you're ready to read about how to study.

YOU CAN DO IT!

Which of these techniques do you already employ? Read the summary to this chapter, and place a check mark next to each statement that describes your approach to college. Then spend a little time thinking about which habits you're willing to develop in your drive to improve your grades. I have also included a few samples of class notes, rewritten notes, and condensed notes.

Here's a sample page from some biology class notes on photosynthesis:

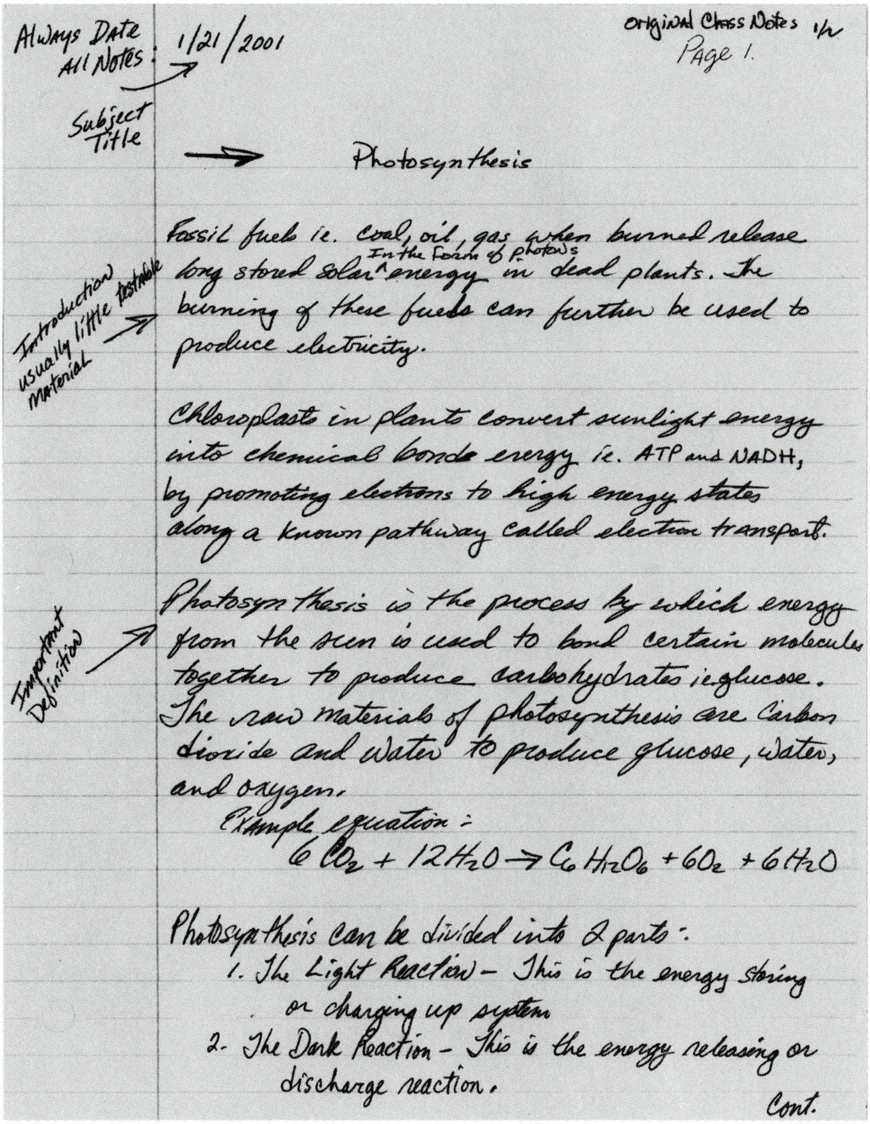

Always Date All Notes: 1/21/2001

Original Class Notes 1/2
Page 1.

Subject Title → Photosynthesis

Introduction usually little testable material →

Fossil fuels ie. coal, oil, gas when burned release long stored solar energy (in the form of photons) in dead plants. The burning of these fuels can further be used to produce electricity.

Chloroplasts in plants convert sunlight energy into chemical bonds energy ie. ATP and NADH, by promoting electrons to high energy states along a known pathway called electron transport.

Important Definition →

Photosynthesis is the process by which energy from the sun is used to bond certain molecules together to produce carbohydrates ie. glucose. The raw materials of photosynthesis are Carbon dioxide and Water to produce glucose, water, and oxygen.

Example equation:

$$6\,CO_2 + 12\,H_2O \rightarrow C_6H_{12}O_6 + 6\,O_2 + 6\,H_2O$$

Photosynthesis can be divided into 2 parts:

1. The Light Reaction – This is the energy storing or charging up system
2. The Dark Reaction – This is the energy releasing or discharge reaction.

Cont.

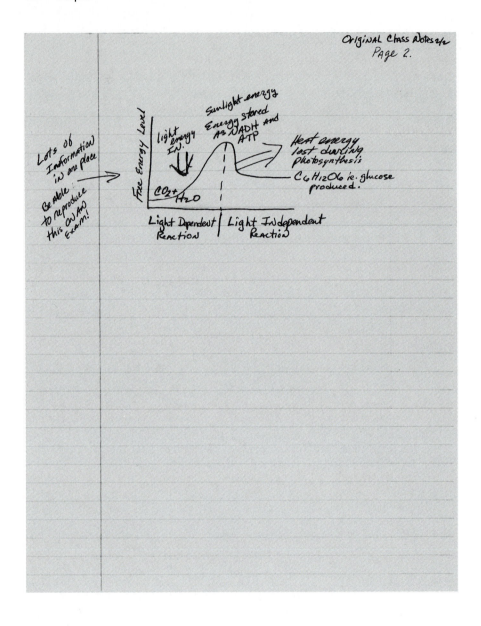

Notice that these notes are sloppy and have broken sentences and poor spelling and grammar. Key words may be scribbled in the margins, and arrows point in various directions. It's a mess. That's why I find it necessary to rewrite my notes; the rewritten notes are easier to read and don't contain repetitious or unimportant information. The process of rewriting notes also helps organize my thoughts.

The rewritten notes might look something like this:

Rewritten Class Notes
Sample #1.

1/21/2001

Photosynthesis

Fossil fuels (oil, gas, coal) release solar
energy stored by ancient plants.

Complete Definition →

Photosynthesis (PS) - process by which
energy of sunlight is used to bond molecules
together to produce the carbohydrate:
glucose. This occurs in chloroplasts and
has the high energy compounds ATP + NADH
which shuffles electrons to the electron transport
chain (An intermediate in PS).

$$6 CO_2 + 12 H_2O \Rightarrow C_6 H_{12} O_6 + 6 O_2 + 6 H_2O$$

Division of (PS): 1. Light dependent reaction - charge up
2. Light independent reaction - run down.

Abbreviate whenever possible

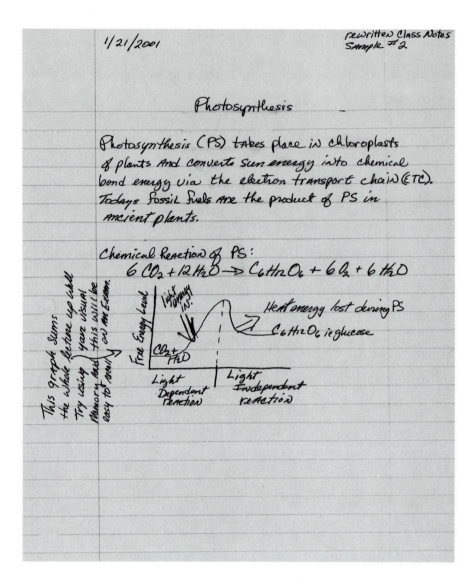

1/21/2001

rewritten Class Notes
Sample #2

Photosynthesis

Photosynthesis (PS) takes place in chloroplasts of plants and converts sun energy into chemical bond energy via the electron transport chain (ETC). Todays fossil fuels are the product of PS in ancient plants.

Chemical Reaction of PS:

$$6 CO_2 + 12 H_2O \rightarrow C_6H_{12}O_6 + 6 O_2 + 6 H_2O$$

This graph sums the whole lecture up well. Try using your visual memory and this will be easy to remember on the Exam.

Free Energy Level

Light energy in.

Heat energy lost during PS

$C_6H_{12}O_6$ ie glucose

$CO_2 + H_2O$

Light Dependent reaction

Light Independent reaction

Notice that the first section of my original notes was an introduction to the lecture and contains little testable material. The next two sections contain repeated material, and I condensed them into one as I rewrote the notes. The chemical equation in the third section makes the last sentence in that paragraph redundant, so I deleted the sentence. Sample #1 leaves the graph out; sample #2 uses the graph, since graphs can be really useful for memorizing a lot of material quickly.

Here are my sample condensed notes.

Always Date to reference
this allows you your original class notes

Definition / formula Sheet

Lec. 1/21 – Photosynthesis – process which converts
sunlight energy (photons) into chemical bond energy
ie. carbohydrate glucose, via electron transport chain
and ATP/NADH. $6CO_2 + 12H_2O \rightarrow C_6H_{12}O_6 + 6O_2 + 6H_2O$.

Do not use complete sentences
they only take up space

Notice that only the most important definitions and equations go on this sheet. New equations and definitions will be added from new lecture notes.

This is the sheet I carry around in my pocket to review two–three times each day or until the material is committed to memory.

8

Making a Pearl from an Irritation: Studying Effectively

Do you know how an oyster makes a pearl? A bit of sand or some other irritant makes its way into the oyster's shell, and the oyster coats the grain of sand with a substance that eventually turns it into a smooth, round pearl. No more irritation for the oyster, and an object of beauty and value for those of us who like pearls.

Studying can be like that—an irritating fact of life that forces its way into the student's shell. The question for you is this: Will you let it continue irritating you, or will you use it to create something of value? In this chapter, I'll tell you what to do with those great sets of notes you've been taking and how to use the textbook, class handouts, and other study materials. I'll also talk about when, where, and how to study, factors that can make more difference that most students imagine.

SET PRIORITIES

Inexperienced students often take a shotgun approach toward their studies. When they find some time in their busy day, they sit down with all their class material in front of them—textbooks, lecture notes, handouts, and homework—and then begin reading aimlessly through the materials. This method is extremely inefficient and usually ineffective because instructors consider some pieces of information more important than others.

You've got to know how to set priorities, and there are several ways to do so. Asking questions and gauging the depth of the response is an excellent technique for determining how important any one source of material might be. For example, you could say, "I'm not sure I understand all the features of the diagram of the circulatory system on page 374. Is there something more I should read?" Casual, offhanded replies signify that the question will not be part of the exam, while in-depth answers are a giveaway that it will be included. If the instructor is vague in reply or will not tell you anything useful, look at previous exams. If no exams are available, be sure you overprepare for your first exam. Don't ever overlook any element of the course that an instructor might rely upon for exam material.

After the first exam, check out the ratio of questions from lecture material to questions from the textbook. You can be fairly certain that ratio will remain constant throughout the course. If the questions run 80 percent lecture material and 20 percent textbook and other materials, allot similar amounts of time to studying: 80 percent to studying lecture notes and 20 percent to reading the textbook.

LECTURE NOTES: SYSTEMATIC REVIEW IS KEY

Let's say you've decided you need to spend 80 percent of your time with your notes for a particular class. What exactly are you going to do with them? After rewriting your daily lecture notes (see Chapter 7), take time to read through all the rewritten and condensed notes that have accumulated since the last examination. I like to do what I call the "three-day-back, one-day-ahead" review. After rewriting the lecture notes for that day, go back and quickly review the past three days of rewritten lecture notes. That's the "three-day-back." Then preview the lecture material (class handouts or reading assignments) for an upcoming lecture. That's the "one-day-ahead." Remember, the lecture you preview should actually be at least three lectures ahead—because you started the semester a week ahead by reading the first chapters in all your textbooks before classes began (see Chapter 7).

For the first few lectures after any examination, reviewing your past lecture notes will take only a short amount of time; little new lecture information will have accumulated. But as another exam draws near, you may be spending up to twenty or thirty minutes reviewing your notes after each class. The time you spend is well worth it. With this consistent, habitual review after each class, you will find that the material becomes firmly committed to memory and may even become difficult to look at again. This is a sign that your hard work is paying off and that you may be confident of doing well on the upcoming exam.

It's common to hear of students who put off studying for exams until a week or less before "the big day." They pride themselves on being able to stay awake for two or three days before an exam and packing in as much as possible of the knowledge they'll need to pass. This imposes an unnecessary amount of stress and loss of sleep on students, leaving them barely conscious by test time; and it makes for a pretty unhappy life in general.

Let's compare the study process to packing a suitcase for a trip. You can take the time needed to fold all your clothes carefully and arrange them so that you will be able to retrieve them easily while you're traveling. I know people who barely need an iron when on the road, and they always look neat and tidy. Or you can simply toss your clothes into a suitcase, slam the lid down, and snap it shut. When you open the suitcase on test day, you discover that in your haste, you only packed one brown sock and one green and all your clothing is too wrinkled to wear; you're not likely to do well on the exam.

My "three-day-back, one-day-ahead" study system doesn't have to take more time than the last-minute approach, either. Let's compare two students. One spends an hour after each class rewriting, organizing, and reviewing the lecture notes. Over a four-week period, this student may spend twenty hours in all reviewing the material from this one class. The other student plans to spend twenty hours during the two days and nights before the test cramming the information into a suitcase-like brain. The students spend the same amount of time studying. Which do you think will get the higher grade? I can guarantee (I know from experience!) that systematic review is both a less painful and a more effective way to pack a suitcase.

Once this "three-day-back, one-day-ahead" system of study and review is working, you will rarely need any extra review sessions. Don't schedule an extra session the night before an exam. Two days before would be better; you can gauge then how your studying has paid off and where you may need some final touches to fill in any gaps in your knowledge. But use this only as a review session; it really isn't a good way to learn new material or study for exams. In Chapter 12 I'll explain exactly what to do the week before the exam.

ASSIGNED HOMEWORK: DO IT!

We are taught to hate homework. The only thing that elicits more groans is a surprise quiz. Under my study system, neither is very fearful.

Many students rack their brains trying to find out what will be on an upcoming test, but the answer is usually quite simple. Test questions are taken from lectures, textbooks, and homework assignments, and often homework is the most telling because it is a synthesis of lecture and textbook information. In many respects, homework is just a practice test that shows off the instructor's preferences and your deficiencies.

There are, of course, some instructors who assign homework primarily to provide you with "enrichment" and who do not consider it to be a critical part of the course. In such a case, do as your conscience and interest dictate—but the homework problems probably won't be on the exam.

In general, however, the importance of assigned homework problems cannot be stressed enough, despite the fact that such assignments are usually not graded. In many college classes, material is introduced during the lecture but you really *learn* it outside of class, often through homework assignments. It is my experience that material learned through doing homework almost certainly will be seen again on an exam. Don't just simply do the assigned homework problems; take the time to understand every detail of the problems and be able to apply their principles to similar problems.

Not grading homework assignments is common in college and is a particular pitfall for students right out of high school who have been taught that anything worth knowing has a grade attached to it. When homework problems are not graded, students often ignore them. In one of my classes, a professor who assigned homework questions but didn't grade them included a number of questions from the homework on an exam. A significant number of students missed those questions, and he realized that the students might not be taking the assignments seriously because he didn't grade them.

Before the next test, he reminded students again that the assigned homework problems were critical to understanding the lecture material and doing well on his exams. On the next exam, he used nothing *but* the homework questions he had assigned. Any student who had completed the homework assignments could have received an extremely easy A. Instead, over half the class failed the exam.

Don't make the same mistake. Most instructors mean exactly what they say and hold you responsible for it. And because many students *don't* do homework, taking it seriously can give you a big advantage.

Homework problems—like lecture notes—should be reviewed throughout the periods between exams. At least once a week, go back and review the various types of homework problems assigned, and commit some sample questions to memory. If homework is assigned daily, I like to study it along with my lecture notes. Each day, after completing an assignment, I go back and review the past three assignments. I don't spend a lot of time on it—maybe ten–fifteen minutes per assignment.

Changing your attitude about homework may be difficult, but it can help catapult you to the top of the class.

CLASS HANDOUTS: WHAT DOES THE INSTRUCTOR THINK IS IMPORTANT?

Whenever an instructor takes the time to bring in an outside source or develops a detailed outline independent of the textbook, pay attention. These are keys to what the instructor believes to be of primary importance, and that's what usually winds up on tests. Incorporate these materials into your regular review process. It's common for an instructor to supplement the lecture material with a handout that illustrates a particular point; and it's almost a sure bet that in some way, material from that handout will be on the exam. So pay particular attention to this supplemental material.

THE TEXTBOOK: SOMETIMES USEFUL, SOMETIMES NOT

The importance of textbooks varies from class to class. Some professors make them an integral part of their lesson plans. Others use them only as supplemental material for students. Right at the beginning of the class, pin the teacher down on use of the textbook. Just ask, How important is the textbook in this course? What percentage of exam material comes from the textbook versus the lecture notes?

When you look at the number of pages assigned, you may think there is no way you could read and memorize this amount of text along with the lecture material, especially if you're taking three or four other classes that require reading. Don't panic. Look at some old exams, or find someone who has taken the class before you and ask them how much the instructor relied on the textbook for exam material. You may find that exam material comes directly from lecture notes, homework, and handouts.

Once you've gauged the importance of the textbook, factor this into your study routine. In general, use the textbook to preview the lecture material as part of the "three-day-back, one-day-ahead" study method. Skim the material relating to the upcoming lecture before each class. This should take very little time. Pay particular attention to headings, bold or underlined print, diagrams, and figures.

If you have an instructor who relies heavily on the textbook, you may need to follow this skimming by a more thorough reading of the material—and even by preexam reviews. Reading the sections related to lecture material again *after* the lecture provides a review, fills in gaps, and can give you a different angle on the same information.

Be an active reader, not a passive one; look for key sections of the reading assignment. Often textbooks have good summaries at the end of every chapter, and you can concentrate on those to be sure you're getting the main points. You may want to use the textbook to fill in gaps in your notes (or your understanding). But it's probably not a good idea to spend a disproportionate amount of time reading and trying to understand every detail in the textbook until you've put a considerable amount of time into understanding your lecture notes.

OLD EXAMS ARE TREASURE MAPS

Instructors who teach the same courses year after year may use very similar exam questions year after year, or at least similar types of questions. Old exams can be used as practice for the real thing, but reviewing exams given in previous semesters a few weeks or even a month or more *before* an exam can also be useful. I do this for a couple of reasons. First, it gives me a feel for what the instructor thinks is the most important material being presented in the class. Second, it gives me an idea about how much detail an instructor expects me to know. This type of information early in the course can help you tailor your studies so as to get the best results on exams and can also save you lots of time.

Some say there are ethical questions about the use of old exams, and of course at colleges where such use is defined as an honor-code violation, you should not use them. But at many schools, instructors keep a file of old exams or put them on reserve at the library specifically for students to review. In Chapter 12, I'll discuss the ethical questions, how to find old exams, and how to use them to prepare for your exam.

WHERE SHOULD YOU STUDY?

Most people need a place to study that offers few distractions. Roommates can be a problem, so many students do most of their studying away from home. Noisy dormitories can also be a problem, so I recommend that you find an alternative study spot or use headphones or earplugs to dampen or completely block the noise. The library is an obvious choice, but if you're a night owl or an extremely early riser, not all libraries will be open at the hours you want to study—and not all libraries are quiet and undistracting.

While it's important to be comfortable, don't make the mistake of thinking you can study only in "the right place." Empty classrooms just down the hall from your next lecture, a quiet corner of a lounge, and student-union snack bars during off-hours are all possible candidates. And don't make the mistake of thinking that you have to be somewhere for a long time to study. You can study in your car at stoplights, in the dining hall at lunch, and in your seat before the lecture begins.

One other important factor: Find a place with proper lighting. Eyestrain is one of the chief causes of fatigue and causes many students to cut their daily study time short. Just as the head lets go of the most heat in winter, the eyes let loose of the most energy; and bad lighting can sop up your energy like a paper towel.

WHEN SHOULD YOU STUDY?

The obvious answer to this question is, of course, every day. The whole point of my study system is to keep up with—to keep *ahead in*—all your classes so that you don't have to panic and cram the night before an exam.

But let's get a little more specific. The time of day you choose to study can make a significant difference in your ability to concentrate. While everyone has a preference—and some people claim they simply cannot function until late in the day—a schedule that seems to work well for many students is to accomplish the bulk of their studies early in the morning. The reason for this is that by the end of a long day of classes or work, the body and mind are tired and ready to relax. Under these circumstances, it can be very difficult to comprehend the more difficult class material, and the student can be easily sidetracked with non-school-related projects. Studying in the morning will let you do your most difficult work when you have the most intellectual energy and physical strength.

Morning study is also a good way to open your brain up to learning. This springboard into the day sets your attitude: School is your job, and you're here to study. When a hypnotist tells the audience what it is going to see, the audience looks for anything that remotely resembles what they were told they would see. Similarly, when you go over your daily outline and preview the course material for that day, you're telling your brain that it is going to learn these things. Like the faithful Igor from Dr. Frankenstein's laboratory, the brain says "yes, Master." As your own hypnotist, you're preparing yourself to expect to study and learn all day.

While class lectures are important, I think you need more energy to study than to go to class. My preference for morning study means that I usually schedule my classes as late in the afternoon or evening as possible. This allows me to study hard in the morning when my mind is fresh. By afternoon, when my mind is fried and I feel like taking the evening off, I just go to class, relax, and take notes. This kind of scheduling forces me to make good use of my time and is really great for motivation.

A few more benefits of morning study: If something I want to do outside of school comes up later in the day (for example, an invitation to a movie), my studies have already been done and I can have fun without jeopardizing my grade. And if you do your studying really early, you may not have to worry about a noisy dormitory; everyone else will be asleep.

The bottom line is to study in the morning when your mind is more ready to absorb new material. It has worked for me and for many others. Get up early and dive into your studies before you embark on anything else. This will assure you that your studies get done—one of the most important factors in achieving top grades in college.

Those of you who insist you just can't function before 11 a.m. might consider night school. Or maybe the opposite would be better for you: Schedule all your classes early in the day, which would force you to get up, and do your studying later in the day, when your brain is functioning at its best.

A FEW MORE STUDY TIPS

Taking breaks while you study is important. The actual time that works best for you may vary, but taking a break allows what you've been reading or studying to sink in. Lots of students seem to think that while they're on a roll, they should keep studying, but it's not the most effective way to retain what you're studying. My personal preference for longer study sessions is to take a ten-minute break after the first two hours of studying and then a five-minute break after each additional hour. The problem with breaks, of course, is that many people have trouble disciplining themselves to get started again. Make sure your ten-minute break doesn't turn into twenty minutes or an hour.

If you come to something you don't understand while you're reading or studying, skip it and come back to it later. This allows your subconscious time to deal with whatever is blocking your understanding. It also reduces anxiety and helps you avoid needless loss of energy from beating your head against the problem. But be sure you make a note of it so that you'll remember to come back to it later or clear it up with your instructor; you may be sorry if you don't.

Do your reviews before starting the new reading or homework assignment for the day. This serves both to warm up your brain by feeding it something familiar and to facilitate linkages and associations between the old material and the new, another plus at exam time when questions may draw on information presented at any time during the semester.

Constant and frequent review is critical. It's okay to shift around your before-exam reviews, but your daily reviews should be stuck to religiously. Don't put them off; don't fall behind. It's the fact that you do them *every day* that makes them effective.

SUMMARY

A common complaint of students is that there isn't enough time in the day to study. Studying effectively may allow you to spend less total time at your studies and get far better grades. In this chapter, I suggested the following:

☆ Use the "three-day-back, one-day-ahead" study method.
☆ Stay ahead in all your classes—never fall behind.
☆ Do all homework problems, even if they're not graded, and include them in your review sessions.
☆ View class handouts as a clear indication of what the instructor sees as important material.
☆ Temper your use of the textbook according to how valuable a source of exam questions it seems to be. In general, use it to preview lecture material, to provide a different perspective on information, and to fill in gaps in your notes.
☆ Find old exams early in the semester and use them to tailor your studying.
☆ Get the biggest portion of your studying out of the way in the morning, and do it in a place that is quiet and well-lighted.

☆ Take frequent short study breaks, but be sure your ten-minute break doesn't turn into twenty minutes.

☆ Be sure to do your reviews every day, and review old material before beginning homework assignments or previewing lecture material.

YOU CAN DO IT!

Let's practice what I've preached here by assessing how important various materials are for just one of your courses.

Course title: You choose the courses.

Indicate whether each of the following is critical, very important, somewhat important, not very important, or not at all important to the course:

Lecture notes
Textbook reading assignments
Class handouts
Homework problems

Let's assess your study habits, too. Answer these questions honestly:

When do you study?
Where do you study?
Do you take study breaks?
Do you use a "three-day-back, one-day-ahead" review system?
How might you modify your study habits now that you've read this chapter?

9

Hitting the Target: Tailoring Your Study to Specific Courses

In the last few chapters, you've learned all the basic study skills that I used to become an A student. But don't you have to study differently for different types of courses? You do. Fortunately, despite the almost infinite variety of courses available at colleges and universities around the country, most of them fall into several categories. In this chapter, I'll give you a sample class schedule and describe how different courses should be approached.

SAMPLE CLASS SCHEDULE

The selection of classes in my sample schedule is arbitrary, but each is representative of a more general category of study, and my study techniques apply to all the classes in that category. For example, while an English composition course requires some unique skills and study habits, it can also be classified as a *Mostly Writing* class—that is, you'll spend most of your study time for this class preparing papers, and your grade will depend primarily on your writing. The other classes in my sample schedule fall into the general categories of *Mostly Reading, Mostly Lecture, Mostly Homework,* or *Mostly Lab Work.* For all classes, my general study tips (see Chapters 7 and 8) apply. In this chapter, I'll focus on what each particular category of class will demand from you and how to apply my study approach to each.

Below is a sample semester schedule for a freshman biology major, but the class descriptions offer something for everyone, no matter what your major is. See Chapter 4 for more information about planning your semester schedule.

Class	Units	Days	Time
English Composition	3	T,Th	1–2:30 p.m.
General Biology (lecture)	3	M,W,F	9–10 a.m.
General Biology (lab)	2	M,W	1–4 p.m.
Calculus	4	M,T,W,Th	8–9 a.m.
Philosophy	3	T,Th	9:30–11 a.m.

While this may be completely different from any semester of college you ever have, it can be used to illustrate the application of methods of study I've detailed in previous chapters. Each class has its own pitfalls and dangers. Remember, the object is to accomplish *your* educational goals while doing what the college expects, and to do both well enough to earn straight A's. With that in mind, take a look at the following classes and what you can expect from each of them.

Mostly Writing: English Composition

The ability to communicate clearly through written language is a highly sought-after skill. It is essential to write well if you want to move to the top of any field. This is not a course to just "get through"; really go after it, and take each writing assignment to heart.

In this type of class, students are expected to write papers on specific subjects. In English composition courses, these papers are graded primarily on grammar, structure, accuracy of citings, and the sources of materials used to compose the paper. On the first day of class, students are told how many papers are required, the tentative due dates of the papers, the lengths expected, and the nature of each. If these specifics are not provided, remember to use the instructor as a resource. You may also have to do quite a bit of reading for classes that teach writing; freshman composition students typically do lots of reading in order to learn how to write. Ask for details about what the class will require. You can't be prepared if you don't know.

What other classes might fall into the *Mostly Writing* category? Any number of English and communications courses—such as technical writing and journalism—and lots of upper-level courses in a variety of fields may require quite a bit of writing. If this is a special concern for you, be sure to find out before registering for a class how much writing is involved—not so that you can avoid the class, but simply to avoid taking too many Mostly Writing classes during one semester. The course catalog, the instructor, and students who have taken the course are all good sources of information.

It is a good idea to start thinking immediately about possible topics, sources, and structure for each paper. Start laying the groundwork for each paper as soon as possible, and plan on finishing each paper well before the due date for the following reasons:

1. Assignment due dates and exams have an uncanny way of coinciding. Your science classes will probably schedule midterm and final exams at about the same time your English composition papers are due. Do you want to be proofreading for typos while you're trying to memorize fungal life cycles? You have to take the exam the day it's given, but you can have that paper done well ahead of time.
2. Many students arrive at college with little or no writing experience, and the prospect of writing several papers for an English composition class is terrifying. If this is you, you definitely have to start on your English papers early so you won't be overwhelmed by the task, frozen by fear, or unable to seek help in time to get it. Starting early gives you time to head for the writing center for help (see Special Topics at the end of the book).
3. If you complete your paper several days or a week early, your instructor may be willing to review it and make suggestions for improving it—and allow you to make the changes before actually turning it in for a grade. Don't be afraid to ask! Your goal is to learn to write a good paper, and the instructor's goal ought to be the same. You can't get a preview on the day the paper's due; you'll get comments when it's returned to you, but usually in red ink.

While I can't teach you how to write a term paper, essay, or composition, I can give you some general hints that might help you in your Mostly Writing classes.

◆ Assume that several drafts will be necessary to reach the finished product. Professional writers don't just sit down and pound out perfect paragraphs; they spend lots of time revising, rewriting, and correcting their own first (and second and third and . . .) attempts.
◆ "Writer's block" is a common malady among students and others. If you find yourself unable to get started on a writing assignment, remember that whatever you first write will be corrected and revised

later. If you can accept the fact that you'll make mistakes and that you'll correct them on the next draft, you'll have less of the fear that can cause writer's block. If you're still unable to get going, seek help from your instructor or the campus writing center. Even prize-winning authors suffer from writer's block. You're not alone.

◆ Check and double-check your paper before you hand it in. Better yet, ask the instructor for comments before the due date, as I mentioned above. If that's not an option, ask a friend or classmate to proofread and review the paper for you. While you need to proofread it yourself, the final check should be done by someone who hasn't read it before. Mistakes that you've missed ten times may be seen on the first read-through by a fresh pair of eyes.

◆ Some English composition and technical writing instructors allow and sometimes even encourage students to write papers that also are required for another class. For example, if you have to write a paper for philosophy, you may be able to have it graded for writing ability in your English composition class. Even if the instructor doesn't mention this possibility, it doesn't hurt to ask. This can really help improve your grade in both classes; you'll be motivated both to do the appropriate research and to write well.

Writing papers can be more time-consuming than you might imagine. But by beginning early and working ahead of deadlines, you'll be learning and working throughout the semester instead of letting all the assignments pile up at the end.

Mostly Lecture, Mostly Lab Work: General Biology Lecture and Lab

This is an example of an undergraduate five-unit science course, with three units Mostly Lecture and two units Mostly Lab Work. A lecture is usually given three times a week for an hour each session, while the lab may meet two or three times a week for two or three hours each time. Another common configuration is the four-unit course, with one unit for a lab that meets once or twice a week.

Other classes that fall into the Mostly Lecture category are most lower-level social science, history, and geography courses. Mostly Lab Work courses typically are labeled "lab" at the freshman and sophomore levels (for example, physics lab, chemistry lab, organic chemistry lab), but at the upper levels you may find labs "hidden" in classes. Read the course catalog carefully, or ask instructors ahead of time whether a class includes a lab.

Lecture-lab courses typically complement one another. While the material covered in each may not always be synchronized exactly with that in the other, and the instructors may not be the same, the lecture material is almost always demonstrated further and supported by the lab exercises and material, and vice versa. When you study for your lab, you are often going over elements of your lecture information—and that can help stick those fur balls of knowledge to the Velcro wall in your brain.

For the lecture portion of the class, follow my previous advice about attending lectures, taking good notes, and reviewing them (Chapters 7 and 8). Always attend lectures, and participate actively by asking questions and seeking clarification on any material you don't understand. The materials and resources available to supplement in-class lectures include the textbook, lecture outlines, assigned homework questions, and handouts from the instructor.

As discussed in Chapter 8, the value of the textbook to a particular class depends on the instructor. But make sure to at least read the assigned pages before class and review the material that you need to have clarified after the lecture.

Some instructors provide detailed outlines of their lectures or supply other material with information not in the textbook. Pay particular attention to these because they rank next to your own lecture notes as a primary source for exam questions. Become familiar with lecture notes, outlines, and handouts as early as possible. Don't wait until the day before class to look at a handout pertaining to the next lecture.

I've said it before and I'll say it again: *Never skip a lecture, and never fall behind.*

Laboratory classes are usually set up to support and clarify lecture material, taking a hands-on approach. More often than not, the information for these classes is contained in a lab textbook that details various experiments or exercises to be carried out by the student.

Read the lab material before class. There is nothing harder than going into a lab cold. I like to create an outline in diagram form—a sketch, really, of the lab procedure. This can include the steps to take, the quantities and types of materials to use, and the questions to answer. This makes the lab go much more smoothly. You're not going to be learning much if you're in a panic about figuring out what in the world to do with those little test tubes and scoops.

I also try to capture the theory behind the experiment and the significance of and reason for performing each step along the way. If this seems like a lot of work, consider that these are the kinds of questions that are most likely to appear on a lab exam.

Lab classes often last two, three, or even four hours although the actual experiment or exercise requires less time than that. In almost every lab class I've had, the majority of students rushed through the lab exercise as quickly as possible—without any effort to understand the reasoning behind it—and then left. Their only goal was to finish the experiment and move on to something else, with the intent of going back and attempting to understand the lab material closer to exam time.

This is a big mistake. One of the keys to becoming a top student is keeping up with the class material. Just doing the work is not keeping up; keeping up with a class means understanding the material presented in it, and a lab presents a great opportunity for doing that. A lab allows you time to ask the instructor questions about difficult material, and it creates a structure in which concepts can build on one another. Stay until the class is over, and use the time wisely.

A note on lab partners: More often than not, you will work with another student or students in a lab course. Usually you can select your partner. Do this carefully. You want to work with someone who takes the lab as seriously as you do. Stay away from people who resist or resent learning or who look at labs as a time to relax and clown around. It may be hard to find someone who matches your commitment—or what I expect your commitment to be once you finish this book—but you need someone who is at least committed to attending all the classes and putting a reasonable amount of effort into doing the experiments. On the other hand, avoid those who are so zealous that they insist on doing all the work; they won't be there when it is test time. And avoid the trap of having a lab partner who thinks you should wash the glassware and take the notes instead of doing the interesting work. This can be a problem for females in particular; there is still a tendency in science classes for males to try to take over. But in a lab, you learn by doing, not by sitting and watching—so assert yourself!

Mostly Homework: Calculus

Calculus is a Mostly Homework class, in which the homework problems assigned are critical to your understanding of course material—and also to your grade. Even if the assignments themselves are not graded, getting an A is probably not possible without doing them. The difference between high school and college is more obvious in this type of class. In college, the instructor introduces the concept, but you have to internalize it outside of class. Trigonometry and algebra are also obviously in this category. Less obvious examples are upper-level methods courses (for example, methods of secondary education, methods of social science research) and statistics, organic chemistry, economics, and computer science courses.

Mostly Homework classes can be very time-consuming. They generally are classes for which the textbook is absolutely vital. Lectures tend to be drawn from the book, as are the daily homework assignments. As always, take comprehensive notes during the lecture. For most people, it takes time for math principles to sink in, especially some of the finer details. Complete lecture notes are a key component of your game plan for conquering math at home.

The habit of reading over textbook material relating to the next lecture really helps in a math class. Don't worry if what you read doesn't make a lot of sense; that's the instructor's job during the lecture. But it will help you follow, and reduce your fear, if you are at least somewhat familiar with the material being presented. After the lecture, read that section of the textbook again, putting more emphasis on understanding the material you missed the first time through or in lecture. Then review your notes from the lecture. (Of course, these are good habits to get into for any course—see Chapters 7 and 8.) Some things will fall into place during this second reading while others will still elude you; but go ahead and start the homework problems.

Most math instructors grade homework. Regardless of the grade value, though, always do all the homework. It's valuable practice for the upcoming exam. And, by all means, if you don't feel that the assigned homework problems have done the job for you, do additional, *unassigned* problems. If you have to think about what you're doing, you probably haven't done enough work; you need to keep working problems until they almost do themselves. Often the answers to at least some of the questions in the book are listed in the back or in a supplemental manual. If you don't have the answers to additional problems, ask your instructor for them.

I like to review homework in the same manner as lecture notes: Each day I go back and review two or three past problem sets to remind myself how to do them. Problems that are second nature to a student solve themselves easily during exams—and they *can* become second nature if you review consistently instead of breezing over them the night before an exam.

Mostly Reading: Philosophy

I categorize philosophy as a Mostly Reading class; that doesn't mean there aren't lectures, but often the lecture hour is spent discussing outside readings. Other examples of Mostly Reading classes are literature courses; many upper-level social science courses; foreign language courses; and even some biology, chemistry, or physics courses. Mostly Reading courses may also require lots of writing, as in a literature class in which the student has a great deal of reading to do and also has to write literary analysis papers.

Typically, the reading in these classes is what I call "nontextbook." Instead of poring over textbook-organized descriptions of philosophers, you'll probably be reading the original works of the philosophers themselves (or works of literature, literary criticism, a treatise on evolution, or whatever). The reading schedule can seem fairly heavy, especially if you've come from a high school that didn't expect much reading; and the reading of original works is definitely different from reading textbooks. For some students, it is more fun and interesting; but for others, it is more difficult and confusing. If you find yourself floundering in your first nontextbook reading class, ask the instructor for help. They know that many students have not been exposed to original works before.

In the humanities, there often are no set answers waiting, and possibly even no set questions. Be sure you understand what your instructors' "contracts" entail (see Chapter 5) and what they expect from their A students. Then get to work. Read, read, read. Attend every lecture. Listen carefully to the instructors: What are their opinions about this piece of work or this philosopher? Take good notes, and review them often. If you begin to feel lost, do something about it before it's a hopeless case. And don't fall behind—you can't hope to read a thousand pages the night before an exam.

Mostly Reading courses typically require much more than just retention; you have to be able to make sense of what you read and to analyze and evaluate it. This suggestion might sound crazy, but if you're having trouble, ask the instructor for *more* to read. Is there something you could read that "translates" Plato's ideas? Are there guides available to help students understand basic ideas? But don't substitute such guides for the real thing; it's important to learn how to read original material, and to make sense of it, yourself.

Often your grade in these classes will depend partly on your class participation; that should be made clear by the instructor. And often the reason instructors make class participation part of a grade is that if they didn't, some students would never say anything. For some reason, many students are reluctant to speak up in class; don't let this reluctance infect you. In a class where your grade, and your learning, is affected by your participation, you need to participate. Don't worry about being flashy or brilliant. (In fact, don't try it—you'll probably fall on your face.) Do make an honest effort to learn about the subject under discussion. Ask questions. Answer questions. Speculate out loud. If you don't understand what you've read, ask specific questions that will help you understand. Don't worry about being naive, either; often a fresh perspective brings new insight to an ancient subject. This is what learning is all about, and in this kind of class, it may also be what your grade is based on.

Mostly Reading classes often have Mostly Writing exams—that is, essay exams (see Chapter 13). Again, if you haven't had much experience expressing yourself through writing, now is the time to learn. If you know the material but can't get any of your ideas on paper, you're in big trouble. See Special Topics for sources of help.

SUMMARY

The general study tips I've provided in other chapters can be applied to all course work, but special techniques may help you do better in particular courses.

☆ Categorize your classes as *Mostly Writing, Mostly Reading, Mostly Homework, Mostly Lecture,* or *Mostly Lab Work.*

☆ Apply my specific study tips to each type of class to tailor your studying to meet the demands made by courses in that category:

1. *Mostly Writing*: Start thinking immediately about each assigned paper with regard to its topic, sources, and structure. Begin laying the groundwork for each paper as soon as possible, and plan on finishing each paper well before the due date. Seek help from the instructor or the campus writing center early in the course if you feel you'll have trouble.
2. *Mostly Lecture:* Follow my previous advice about attending lectures, taking good notes, and reviewing notes (Chapters 7 and 8).
3. *Mostly Lab Work:* Read the lab material before the class. Create an outline in diagram form—a sketch of the lab procedure. Try to capture the theory behind the experiment and the significance of and reason for performing each step along the way. Stay until the class is over, and use the lab time wisely. Select your lab partner carefully.
4. *Mostly Homework:* Read over textbook material relating to the next lecture. Always do all the homework. In order to practice more difficult material, do additional problems not assigned. Review homework in the same manner as lecture notes: Review two or three past problem sets each day.
5. *Mostly Reading:* Read, read, and read. Attend every lecture. You

have to learn to make sense of what you read and to analyze and evaluate it; listen carefully to the instructor for this kind of information. Take good notes, and review them often. If you find yourself floundering in your first nontextbook reading class, ask the instructor for help.

YOU CAN DO IT!

List the courses you're taking this semester. Now assign each to one of the categories listed in this chapter. Using the summary, compare your current approaches to the classes with my recommendations. Are you satisfied with your work in each course? How could you use the tips in this chapter to improve your grades?

10

Time Waits for No Student: Sample Study Schedule and a Guide to Managing Your Time

Why do so many students spend their time desperately trying to catch up—handing assignments in late and cramming for exams the night before? Why is pulling an all-nighter something nearly every college student knows about? Because almost no one manages time well. If you are among the few students who do, you'll go a long way toward your goal of getting straight A's. One of the most basic steps you can take toward becoming a top student is to get ahead of the class and stay ahead. *Never fall behind!*

I worked hard to become a straight-A student. But because I used the study methods in this book, I could call it quits by 7 p.m. or at least 8 p.m. every evening. In this chapter, I'll tell you how I organized my time and provide lots of tips to help you manage yours.

HOW MUCH TIME DO YOU HAVE?

From the moment you enroll, you have a fixed amount of time to do everything necessary to lay the educational foundation for the rest of your life. Let's take a look at how much time you're going to invest in your undergraduate education—and how you should use that time.

The average school year is nine months long. Without breaking that time into semesters, quarters, or other units, multiply that nine months by the thirty days in a month. This gives you roughly 270 days a year in which to attend class, study your lessons, review your lecture notes, do your homework, and take a few tests. Seems like a lot of time, doesn't it? It seems like even more when you multiply those 270 days by the twenty-four hours in a day. You have 6,480 hours to finish a single year of school! Piece of cake, right? That's what most students think, and off they go to the football game.

But let's look at how you use those 6,480 hours. Maybe you'll get to average six hours sleep a night; you really should shoot for more, but let's use that number. You've just lost 25 percent of your hours—that's 1,620 hours, gone in dreamland. But you still have 4,860 hours left for school. Shouldn't be too hard, right? You say you need to eat? Between preparing food and driving to McDonald's, you spend at least another two hours a day on food. That's right—there go another 540 hours, and we haven't even cracked a book yet. Of the 4,320 hours remaining, most students will spend at least an hour a day on little details like showering, dressing, and combing their hair. That means we're down to 4,050 hours, and we still haven't done any studying or even seen a teacher. You use a minimum of nine hours a day to accomplish things that have absolutely nothing to do with school. And what about the student who has to work part- or full-time, or the one who's taking care of a family, or the one who's participating in college athletics? If you have even more demands on your nonschool time than I've described here, you *really* need to learn to manage your time.

Now let's go to school and see what happens to your time. If you're taking a sixteen-hour load per week, which is fairly typical, you can plan on spending 624 hours a year in a classroom. That leaves you under 3,500 hours to study, review, and take tests. If you spend two hours studying for each hour you spend in class, you can kiss another 1,248 hours good-bye.

The point is this: The time that looms so large at the beginning of the school year isn't really all there for you to devote to your studies. In fact, of the total we started with, less than a third is left as discretionary time. How are you going to use it? Gazing out the library window daydreaming, sleeping off hangovers, and cramming in panic for exams? Or becoming an A student? It's up to you.

MAKING A STUDY SCHEDULE

With so little time available, how are you going to accomplish all the work you'll have to do to get straight A's? What you need is a study schedule. In fact, you need *two* study schedules: one that maps out the whole semester, to remind you of upcoming exams, paper due dates, and the like; and another daily study schedule that gives you a list of work for every day. There are a variety of ways to create these schedules.

Paul developed a simple scheduling program on his computer that allows him to print out his study plan for the week. He uses that plan to organize his day and keep himself on track. His program also tracks the dates of exams and paper and report due dates. If this seems like overkill, understand that when Paul finishes studying at 7 p.m. every evening, he's finished studying! Many of the students I know don't start until then.

Perhaps you don't have a computer that allows you to make a schedule and fill it in so comprehensively. A friend who is the administrator at an adult school happened to open his date book when I was with him once, and I had to laugh. The book was made up of blank calendar pages without numbers. He photocopies the blank and then fills in the dates and days himself.

"I was poor all my life and didn't want to spend money on new appointment calendars," he told me. "But I've also found that when I put in the dates and days myself, I have a much better grasp of the day-to-day flow of the month."

The moral of this little tale is that you don't need an expensive computer or fancy date book to keep yourself on schedule. *You* are the one who determines how much attention you pay to your plans, and you'll be more likely to use a study schedule you are comfortable with.

Here's how I do it: Each evening before closing my books, I take a few minutes to outline my study goals for the next day. This is a very personal habit, but it's one that really prepares me for my early morning study session and for the rest of the day. Your goals should be set slightly beyond your grasp; this will create a constant pressure to try harder. By setting goals each day, you'll be challenged constantly—by yourself.

I like to keep this goal list simple and carry it in my shirt pocket where it is readily available to remind me of my daily ambitions. The list should address what is to be accomplished the next day in class. Based on the sample class schedule discussed in the last chapter, a goal list might look like this:

English: Find three articles in the library for paper on handgun control.

Biology (lecture): Rewrite today's lecture notes in condensed form; review the past three days of condensed lecture notes; skim tomorrow's lecture topic in textbook.

Biology (lab): Read and outline lab exercise for following class lab.
Calculus: Review today's class lecture notes: review past three days'
homework and lecture notes; do homework assignment.
Philosophy: Read Aristotle's discussion of the lack of justice in the
educational system.

While this list seems to detail a lot of work, most of the items can be completed in fifteen–twenty or twenty–thirty minutes. The math homework assignment, which should be done slowly and methodically, may take longer. The reviews scheduled in math and biology should be done quickly—just read-throughs (see Chapter 8).

I refer to this study list throughout the day and mark off items as I complete them. When I'm really pressed, I try to include a specific time to complete each task instead of just consulting the list every time I have a free moment. At the end of each day, I make sure everything on my study schedule is marked off, and I write up my next day's study plan on the same piece of paper. (If I have really set my goals too high, some items will have to be carried over to the next day.) Then, at the beginning of the week, I start over again with a new piece of paper. If my class schedule was like the one in Chapter 9, my study schedule at the end of a week might look like this:

Monday (Calculus 8–9, General Biology 9–10, GB lab 1– 4)
Calculus: Do today's homework; preview tomorrow's lecture in text-
book; review the past three lectures/homework.
Biology (lecture): Rewrite today's lecture notes; preview Wed. lec-
ture in textbook.
Biology (lab): Review today's lab; preview Wed. lab.
English composition: Skip today.
Philosophy: Preview Tues. lecture materials.

Tuesday (Calculus 8–9, Philosophy 9:30–11, English 1– 2:30)
Calculus: Do today's homework; preview tomorrow's lecture in text-
book.
Biology (lecture): Review past three lectures; preview Fri. lecture
in textbook.
Biology (lab): Skip today.

English composition: Read class assignment; finish sample outline.
Philosophy: Review/rewrite today's lecture notes; preview Thurs. lecture materials; read Aristotle assignment.

Wednesday (Calculus 8–9, General Biology 9–10, GB lab 1–4)
Calculus: Do today's homework; preview tomorrow's lecture in textbook; review past three lectures.
Biology (lecture): Rewrite/review today's lecture notes.
Biology (lab): Review today's lab; preview Mon. lab; work on lab report.
English composition: Skip today.
Philosophy: Skip today.

Thursday (Calculus 8–9, Philosophy 9:30–11, English 1–2:30)
Calculus: Do today's homework; preview Mon. lecture in textbook.
Biology (lecture): Review past three lectures; preview Mon. lecture in textbook.
Biology (lab): Skip today.
English composition: Decide on paper topics; sketch out outlines.
Philosophy: Review/rewrite today's lecture notes; read next assignment.

Friday (General Biology 9–10)
Calculus: Preview Tues. lecture in textbook.
Biology (lecture): Review past three lectures; preview Mon. lecture.
Biology (lab): Preview next Wed. lab; review last three labs; work on lab report.
English: Find three articles in the library for paper on gun control.
Philosophy: Preview next Tues. lecture materials.

Saturday (no classes)
Calculus: Review last week's lectures/homework assignments; preview next Wed. lecture in textbook.
Biology (lecture): Skip today.

Biology (lab): Skip today.
English: Take notes on articles; outline handgun-control paper; think about introduction.
Philosophy: Skip today.

Sunday (no classes)
Calculus: Skip today.
Biology (lecture): Review past week's lectures.
Biology (lab): Skip today.
English: Skip today.
Philosophy: Review past week's lectures; work on researching/writing paper; read next assignment.

The above is an example of what you might find in my pocket at the end of a week. The only difference is that each day, as I finish a particular item, I cross it out. Keep in mind that this list is not made out a week ahead of time but that each night I make out a list of what I hope to accomplish the next day.

My study schedule illustrates some key points that are elaborated on in other parts of the book.

♦ Notice that I put calculus first each day; this is because it required a graded homework assignment each day.
♦ Notice that for the classes I found harder and more time-consuming—such as calculus and the biology lecture—I scheduled frequent reviews of the past three lectures. This constant review drives a lot of material into your head with little effort or stress.
♦ Notice that in each subject, I'm constantly previewing the material to be covered in future lectures. This is very important. It lets you know where the class is heading and allows you to anticipate problems and ask intelligent questions in class.
♦ Notice that by the end of the week, I already have previewed through Wednesday of the next week for calculus and biology.
♦ Notice that in philosophy and English composition, I have kept up with the classes all week and have worked consistently on papers that are due sometime in the future.
♦ Notice that I skip subjects some days; it's not necessary to put in work on every class every single day. This varies according to your assignments and the days the class meets.
♦ Finally, notice that on the weekend, I have used time to go back

and review the material covered in classes over the entire week and have made sure that I have previewed well into the next week.

Sound like a lot of work? It is. But the students who get A's consistently in college cover class material this thoroughly and put in this much time. Still, it's not as bad as it seems. First, realize that this particular class schedule of fifteen units represents a hard college semester, not an easy one. Second, this sample study schedule is a best-case scenario; some days, with the best intentions, there will be one or two items that you just didn't have time to do.

STUDY WHENEVER YOU CAN

You may still be thinking, "There's no way I could go to classes for several hours each day and then complete all the goals on this list!" I'm not expecting you to finish it all after you get back to your room or apartment in the evening; I'm expecting you to work on it throughout the day. Let's look at your class schedule again. On Mondays and Wednesdays, from 10 a.m.–1 p.m. you have no classes and you get out of school at 4 p.m. On Tuesdays and Thursdays, you have no classes from 9 a.m.–9:30 a.m. or from 11 a.m.–1 p.m. and you get out of school at 2:30 p.m. On Fridays, you have only one class, for one hour; and you have no classes at all on Saturdays and Sundays. When at school, study whenever possible—including before classes and even during lunch. It comes down to a question of doing it now, when you're at school anyway and have some available time; or doing it later, when you are being squeezed up against an exam or wishing you could go to a party or for a hike in the woods. It takes practice, but after a couple of months, or one good semester, it gets a lot easier. Make good use of all that time!

In fact, when you know exactly what you need to do (consult that study schedule), any moment you have free is an opportunity to study. Stalled in traffic? You can turn up the radio and lip-sync, or you can pull out your condensed notes and start scanning. Combing your hair? Why not decorate your mirror with French verb conjugations, mathematical formulas, or the names of British kings so you can review while combing? What are your plans for dinner? Find a way to prop up your book and graze some topics while slurping up your spaghetti.

Making use of all these odd moments, hours between classes, and times stuck in traffic is much easier when you have a study schedule. It takes the debating out of your day; you don't waste time wondering whether you should read an extra chapter in biology or review math problems. As the Nike ad says, "Just do it!" Do whatever is on your list. When you're done, write up tomorrow's list of study goals—and then reward yourself by taking the rest of the night off.

Are you still convinced there's no way you can do all that work in one day? Actually, the only items on this sample schedule that might take a considerable amount of time are the calculus homework assignments each day, and that depends on your math abilities. The constant reviews of past lectures and the previews of future lectures take no more than fifteen–twenty minutes per subject. The purpose of these reviews is not to try to understand or memorize each point in your notes; by reviewing them so frequently, you learn *without* spending hours memorizing. It is necessary only to skim through your notes very quickly—don't spend more than, at most, twenty–thirty minutes reviewing any one thing. What you miss today you'll pick up tomorrow or the next day; that's why you review at least three times. What's important is keeping these lecture reviews consistent and frequent throughout the semester. This is a low-stress way to learn a lot of material. Likewise, by working consistently at your philosophy reading assignments and English paper assignments, you save yourself from panicked marathon reading or writing sessions later in the semester, when you'll be trying desperately to catch up in time to pass the course.

SUMMARY

Time is limited—there's no doubt about that. But the disciplined study habits you'll acquire by using a study schedule create extra time. Here's a quick recap of my suggestions for managing your time:

☆ Use a calendar to keep track of all assignment due dates and exam dates.

☆ Write a list of your study goals every evening based on homework and reading assignments, papers and lab preparations, and upcoming exams.

☆ Refer to the study list throughout your day, and try to cross off every item by the end of the day.

☆ Use every available slot of time during your work day to complete the items on your list.

☆ Don't spend more than fifteen–twenty minutes on your note reviews for each subject.

☆ Be creative in putting odd moments of time to good use.

The sample study schedule I have presented in this chapter—which seems, at first glance, to entail an impossible amount of work—will keep you up to date in all your classes, prevent you from having a truly impossible amount of work to do late in the semester, and provide you with extra opportunities for interacting with instructors. It is an excellent way to learn. Manage your time well—and you're on your way to getting straight A's.

YOU CAN DO IT!

Let's put this information to work by designing a study goal list. List the classes you have tomorrow, and fill in the kinds of work you need to do for each class. Include lecture previews, homework assignments, work on long-term projects such as term papers or research projects, and note reviews. Also, you may want to look over the sample long-term planning calendar at the end of this chapter.

LECTURE - LABORATORY SCHEDULE

COURSE: Chem 12A   **MONTH:** November

MONDAY	TUESDAY	WEDNESDAY	THURSDAY	FRIDAY
	1	**2** Chapter 10	**3**	**4** *Calculus Exam* Chapter 10
	Ch. 9, pp. 108-113 Ch. 10, Exp. 1	Lab Exam 1	Lab Exam 1	
7 Chapter 10	**8** *Meet with Pre-Med. Counselor*	**9** Chapter 10	**10**	**11** VETERAN'S DAY HOLIDAY
Ch. 9, pp. 108-113 Ch. 10, Exp. 1	Ch. 9, pp. 108-113 Ch. 10, Exp. 1	Synthesis of Ethyl phenyl-acetate	Synthesis of Ethyl phenyl-acetate	
14 Chapter 10	**15**	**16** *Meet Shari for Lunch* Chapter 8	**17**	**18**
Synthesis of Ethyl phenyl-acetate	Synthesis of Ethyl phenyl-acetate	Synthesis of Ethyl phenyl-acetate	Synthesis of Ethyl phenyl-acetate	
21 Chapter 8	**22** *History Mid Term*	**23** *English Term Paper Due* Chapter 8	**24** THANKSGIVING HOLIDAY	**25**
Synthesis of Ethyl phenyl-acetate	Synthesis of Ethyl phenyl-acetate	To Be Announced		
28 Chapter 9	**29**	**30** Chapter 9		

Any way you can keep track of all your assignments is OK. One semester, I used a calendar handed out by my organic chemistry instructor and just wrote in all my other obligations and assignments. Lots of students have daily planners; these can be used for keeping track of your assignments and exams as well as for writing your daily goal lists.

11

The Relativity of Grades

One of the most important and often overlooked aspects of improving your grades is understanding what grading is all about. Often students attempt to improve their grades without really knowing how each grade was calculated or what it means. That's putting yourself at a severe disadvantage. How can you improve something you don't fully understand? One of the first steps up the ladder to the top of your class is gaining an understanding of grades. In this chapter, I'll explain the most common grading systems, talk about what goes into final grades, tell you how to keep track of your own grades, and offer a few general suggestions for improving your grades.

WHAT IS A GRADE?

Understanding how instructors assign grades can be key to your study habits. Is it true that some instructors grade papers by tossing them down a flight of steps and giving those that go farthest the highest grades? You sometimes may feel that grades are assigned that arbitrarily. But there are actually two basic approaches to calculating final class grades.

1. Using a traditional grading method, the instructor assigns a numerical value to each student's class performance that reflects the

instructor's experience with the material and with previous students. Letter grades are then assigned based on the following breakdown:

90–100 percent	A
80–89 percent	B
70–79 percent	C
60–69 percent	D
Below 60 percent	F

2. In the curve system, the top grade in each class replaces the 100 percent score as the standard against which all other students are measured. Under the curve system, the differences in exams and in teaching abilities of instructors can be factored out, and different classes of students can be compared. Grading on a curve is considered by many to be one of the fairest grading systems. After all exams or assignments have been graded numerically, the instructor assigns an A to the paper with the highest score, and all the other papers receive letter grades relative to this top score.

Here's a comparison of the two systems. Let's say the highest score on a very difficult chemistry exam was 80 out of a possible 100 points. Under a conventional grading system, papers with scores between 90 and 100 would receive A's, between 80 and 89 would receive B's, between 70 and 79 receive C's, and so forth. That means the best paper in the class would receive a low B. Using a curve system, 80 would become the standard for the class, and students scoring between 90 and 100 percent of 80 would receive A's.

Another method of curving is to give the top and bottom 10 percent of the class A's and F's respectively, the next 15 percent from the top and bottom B's and D's, and the remaining middle portion of the class C's. There are many ways of making up a curve; the common denominator is that students are graded relative to one another instead of being measured against an unyielding standard.

WHAT GOES INTO THE FINAL GRADE?

While there are any number of variations on the grading theme that fall between the conventional and the curve systems, it is probably more important to focus on the ingredients of your final grade than on the exact way in which it will be calculated. As I described in Chapter 5, many instructors tell you exactly what it will take to get an A in their classes. This might include accumulation of quiz and test scores and a factor of homework assignments. Often this "recipe" for your final grade is presented in a chart of the various tests and papers that includes the weight of each. For example:

5 quizzes	25 percent
Midterm exam	25 percent
Final exam	50 percent

These numbers will shift according to the amount of work required or the difficulty involved in the quizzes and exams. Some professors don't like to place too much emphasis on only two tests (the midterm and the final) and so will beef up the value of their quizzes.

An English syllabus might include the following information on figuring your grade:

Essay 1	20 percent
Term paper 1	25 percent
Essay 2	25 percent
Term paper 2	30 percent

Other variations are possible. Some instructors tell their students that an A on the final exam means an A for the course. Others factor your work in class—your participation and your contribution—into your grade. Some have a policy of dropping your lowest exam grade, or allowing you to decide before you take the final whether you'd like to drop your lowest exam grade.

Different types of exams and different types of assignments are graded differently, and you need to be aware of these differences. Sometimes answers on an exam are clearly either right or wrong; other times there may be room for getting partial credit or for misinterpreting both questions and answers. Grading can range from very subjective to very objective. Most multiple-choice exams, for example, are graded by computer; there's not much room for subjectivity there (see Chapter 13 for a detailed discussion of different types of exams). On the other hand, you may get a term paper back some day with a single letter grade on it and no further information about how it was graded. Another instructor may grade you separately on grammar, style, originality, research, and a variety of other criteria, thus giving you a much better idea of why you got the grade you did.

All these possibilities underscore the importance of having a clear understanding of the instructor's goals for his or her students; in a very real way, your fate is in this person's hands. Most instructors provide some sort of statement detailing their expectations in writing. But it is your responsibility to be sure you understand exactly what you need to accomplish in every class to get the grade you want.

KEEP A PERSONAL SCORECARD

Not only is it your responsibility to know what you must do to earn an A, it's your responsibility to keep track of your progress in each class. What I've been talking about throughout this book is taking responsibility for your own actions, and this includes tracking your progress in the classes you take. You ought to be able to judge your performance in the classroom, both on a personal basis and relative to other students in the same class. The grades you get should never be a surprise. If you follow the program presented in this book, you'll start to know very quickly how well you are going to do on a particular test just by flexing your new intellectual muscles. When you invest the right amount of quality time studying for an upcoming test, you pretty well know the outcome, often before you even take the test.

Become your own accountant; keep track of your scores in all your classes. This checking of your "grade pulse" will allow you to know the condition of your grade every step of the way and to take steps to improve it before it's too late. Of course, knowing your grades every step of the way will take all the climax and excitement out of receiving your report card—but you'll probably be thinking about next semester by that time anyway.

CATCH THE DIPS

Let's imagine that you discover your grades are dipping in one or more of your classes. The moment you spot this downward trend, pinpoint the problem and correct it. If you wait too long, you may not be able to catch up. If you detect the first downward swing, it will take less energy to reverse it than if you wait until things have gotten out of control.

Once you notice a dip in your progress, assess the problem. It's possible that certain formulas or types of information are not sticking in your brain, and you may be able to identify these and work harder on them. Put in more hours, check your organization for this particular class, seek help at a campus study center, find out about getting a tutor, or ask the instructor for guidance.

Unfortunately, the natural urge is to swing *away* from the material you're having difficulty with, not to put more energy into it. This is one of the worst pitfalls. When you have a subject cold, you enjoy working with the associated problems because you feel good about your ability. This is exactly the problem. Remember one simple command when it comes to difficult subjects: Seek discomfort. Terrible, isn't it? But when you are uncomfortable with a particular subject, tighten your belt and work to make that subject your best.

When you've realized that you're having a problem in a class but you aren't sure why, or what to do about it, seek help from the instructor. Simply ask, What am I doing wrong? Most instructors will do their best to help you assess your problem. And you don't need to wait for trouble to discuss your progress with your teachers. If you have already established rapport with them, as I suggested earlier in this book, an occasional spot check will help keep you on track. The instructors will already know your goals and will let you know if you are meeting their criteria for your ambition. By keeping close track of your grades and classroom performance, you can catch problems before they seriously affect the outcome of your final class grade.

LEARN FROM ALL MISTAKES

In my experience, the worst test score in any given class is usually the first one. No matter how hard you study, there are always some fine-detail changes you can make in your study strategies to tailor them to each class, and the first exam can help you do so. Analyze the approach you took in studying for this first exam, and change your study techniques to maximize your grade on the next exam.

First exams are critical, but you can learn from your performance elsewhere, too. Go over each test and each graded assignment closely. Looking critically at your mistakes will allow you to continue to improve throughout the semester. Fine tune your study habits to meet the instructor's requirements; always devote your study energies to the information the instructor values the most. This may mean giving more attention to your reading assignments or concentrating more on the material in class handouts or lecture notes. Look at where the test questions came from. Do you need to read more of the text? Are your lecture notes comprehensive enough to get the A you seek?

Once you learn what you can on your own, go to the instructor with the exam or the homework assignment. Make sure that you understand what the instructor expects you to answer. Find out why you got only partial credit for something or how you should have done the homework assignment. The response you get will also tell you more about the instructor, and that will help you get a better grade in the end.

STAY AHEAD OF THE PACK

You stand a much better chance of getting the grades you want if you can unlock the secret of the instructor's grading system—and then aim for someplace *beyond* the top. Getting the top grade means doing *better* than the professor's expectations, and that means the recipe for an A is an intermediary goal. Your target should be somewhat beyond everyone else's.

Sound like more work? You're right. But overshooting the expectations of the professor is the best way to ensure an A. Many unforeseen events pop up during school. You may become ill or encounter personal problems, and it means missing classes. If you're just working at everyone else's pace, you'll fall behind. If you're working *ahead* of the others, it will keep you in the hunt. Though this may be the most overused phony excuse students give instructors, it's possible your grandmother *will* die while you're in school. If you're already weeks behind, or even just barely keeping up, a major problem in your life could pretty much end the semester for you.

Sometimes aiming beyond the top means doing extra credit work in addition to the normal course requirements; for more information on extra credit, see Special Topics at the end of the book.

GIVING UP IN A CLASS

Sometimes you decide that you want to get out of a course you're already registered for. You may feel that it is being poorly taught by a bad instructor, or you may find that you've registered for too many really tough classes in one semester (the class that sounded like fluff in the catalog is going to be more time-consuming than you had imagined). For whatever reason, the class is not going to help you meet your goals. You need to learn to recognize the situations that can jeopardize your grade-point average and to get out before any damage is done.

Several factors need to be considered when deciding whether to drop, withdraw from, or stay in a class. Dropping a class is far preferable to withdrawing from it. While the language may vary from school to school, I'm talking about whether your departure from the class is permanently recorded. A class that is "dropped" early in the semester will usually not show up on your transcript; a "withdrawal" takes place later in the term and will always be part of your transcript. This means that anyone who sees your transcript will know that you started a class but withdrew.

While dropping is preferable to withdrawing, be careful not to drop classes too casually. If you have a plan that will carry you through graduate school, you can't afford to get too far off track. Dropping a class or two seems harmless on the surface, but it can have severe ramifications. When you drop a class after the semester has started, getting into another, more desirable class may be impossible. If your study plan calls for taking certain courses, you'll have to load up a later schedule or settle for courses that do not exactly fit the long-term plan. Also, some later courses may depend on the course you just dropped as a prerequisite for entrance.

If you're tempted to drop a class because of a conflict with your instructor, read Special Topics at the end of the book before you take any action.

SUMMARY

To get the grades you want, you must know exactly what the instructor expects of you and how the instructor's grading system works.

☆ Use the instructor's statement of the course requirements and the "recipe" for the final grade as a guide to help you set your short-term and long-term goals for the course.

☆ Be aware that it's your responsibility to be sure you understand what you need to do to get your A.

☆ Keep track of your progress in all your classes, and work to improve your performance immediately if your grades begin to slip.

☆ Do an occasional check with the instructor throughout the semester to be sure you're on track.

☆ Remember to work hardest in the areas you're least comfortable with.

☆ Work not simply to meet but to exceed the instructor's expectations for an A student.

☆ Don't drop classes too casually, but if you do decide to drop a class, do it early in the semester so that your withdrawal won't be recorded on your transcript.

YOU CAN DO IT!

Do you know what your grades are based on? Take some time right now and use the space here to list your courses and the requirements for each. Be sure you know how many exams, quizzes, papers, and homework assignments are required for each class and how much each assignment contributes to your final grade.

12

While Others Sweat (or, Seven Days Before the Exam)

Using my method of study, you'll keep up with every class throughout the semester and approach each exam with the knowledge that you've put in the work required. In this chapter, I'll tell you how and what to study during the last week before an exam to be sure you're as ready as you can be.

THE CASE AGAINST CRAMMING

It takes a certain amount of time to get an A in any class. If the semester is three months long and a given class takes two hours a day of study to master the material, you'll need a total of 180 hours of study just for that class. My method of study says put in those two hours each day and walk in and take the exams well-prepared, wide-awake, and with confidence.

Instead of following my advice, you could study only one hour per day, leaving you ninety hours to make up in the last seven days before the test. That's twelve hours a day studying for the whole week before the exam. This is truly cramming, and it does work for some people some of the time. Unfortunately, you're not taking just one class, and most midterms and finals arrive around the same time. When you try to make up for lost time during the week before an exam, the problem of cramming is compounded by the number of classes you're taking.

Cramming leads to stress and loss of sleep, both of which drastically affect your ability to absorb the information necessary to pass exams. Stress, in particular, becomes a wall that blocks your ability to remember. When study is a painful endeavor, the mind automatically begins the process of forgetting—at the very moment you need to remember as much as you possibly can.

My experience is that cramming is painful, you don't learn much that sticks with you for more than twenty minutes past the end of the exam, and the results in terms of grades are anything but guaranteed. If you've been paying attention all along as you read this book, you've already opted for the study-every-day alternative.

THE LAST WEEK IN DETAIL

Let's assume you've kept up your study throughout the semester. By now, you've reviewed the class lecture material and homework assignments so many times you're sick of looking at them. In fact, the upcoming exam will be a welcome relief because it will mean you can stop looking at this material. Believe me, this is a great feeling. If you don't need to cram because you've been reviewing all semester, what should you do the last seven days before an exam?

Don't Neglect New Material

Keep doin' what you been doin'! Go to class, take good notes, rewrite your notes, do your homework, and review your notes. I suggest that you put about 70 percent of your time into learning this last week of class material. It's a common mistake to blow off this last week of classes and put time only into the class material already presented. I don't know what it is about the last week of class, but it's been my experience that instructors take a healthy number of test questions from it. So know this material. For the last couple of days of lecture, of course, you won't have the luxury of reviewing your condensed notes lightly over two or three days; spend a little more time than usual memorizing the finer details of this new material.

Of course, if you have good reason to believe this last week of material won't be on the exam, tailor your study time accordingly. But if you knock off class to study for the exam, you'll be that much further behind for the next exam; so at least keep going to class and taking good notes.

Review the Old Material

How about the other 30 percent of your study time? Review past class material, and prepare for the exam. Specifically, I suggest the following:

◆ Pull out your original, noncondensed lecture notes and review them at least once, and preferably twice. Pay particular attention to the finer details of these notes and to any details that didn't make it into your condensed notes. Remember, you've been reviewing those condensed notes throughout the semester, and by now you're sick of looking at them.

◆ Review all old homework assignments. If homework was a considerable part of the class, I suggest that you go over each assignment and choose a few homework problems that represent the main concepts. Make sure you know these sample problems backwards and forwards. Choose a few similar problems that you haven't tried before, and do them as practice.

◆ Review all available old exams. In fact, I recommend that you start working at least two weeks prior to your own test date. If possible, save the most recent exam for a dry run to be self-administered several days before your exam under the same time constraints that will exist on the actual day of the test. While old exams help you determine what the instructor deems the most important points in the class and help you decide where you will focus any extra time you may have to study, they hold no guarantees. Once in a while you may see some questions from an old exam pop up on yours; this is icing on the cake. But you may also find that the next exam bears absolutely no resemblance to the old ones you reviewed.

◆ Look over any reading material that may have been assigned. It's not going to take that much time; "looking over" doesn't mean it's necessary to read all the textbook material again. You've already seen it once. I suggest you thumb through the textbook quickly and "read smart." Pay particular attention to titles, subtitles, bold print, tables, graphs, and chapter summaries. These items stick out like a neon sign to any instructor looking for possible exam questions.

◆ Early in the last week before the exam, stop by your instructor's or teacher aide's office and ask any questions you haven't been able to answer on your own. By doing this early in the week, you will avoid the last-minute rush of your classmates and give yourself time to follow up and study any additional material the session directs you to. Of course, this should not be the first time you've done this. As I mentioned earlier in this book, you should make regular visits to your instructor's office and clear up questions as they arise, but it's particularly important that you do this the week before the exam because it's not uncommon for instructors to make changes related to exams that may alter your study plan. Be on the lookout for possible exam questions. Pay attention to how your instructors answer your questions. How detailed are their answers? What key words do they use? Usually, the way instructors answer *your* questions is a clue to how to answer *their* questions on the exam.

◆ Don't spend a disproportionate amount of time studying material you already know. This is a trap even the best students fall into. After all, it's easier to study material you already know. Reviewing gives you more confidence—but it doesn't pay off on exams. After you've done your initial review of all the material (lecture notes, homework, and so on), spend the rest of your time expanding your horizons of knowledge.

◆ If the instructor offers any review, question, or practice sessions, attend them! And attend them armed with questions you need answered and problems you can't solve. Pay attention at such sessions for clues about what might be on the exam, what will *not* be on the exam, and how the instructor expects you to approach various topics. Instructors hold such sessions to help their students, and often the help is very direct. An instructor might say something like, "That's a very good question" when a student asks something that will be on the exam. So pay close attention to the way the instructor answers questions.

◆ You've kept your nose to the books all semester; you've studied hard. Now take off the night, or even the afternoon, before the exam. Relax. That's right! Reward yourself. You deserve it. Unlike your classmates, you're ready for the exam; all your hard work has come together, and no doubt tomorrow you'll get that A. A relaxed day and a good night's sleep can only help.

BACK TO THE QUESTIONS ABOUT OLD EXAMS

I've already discussed how valuable I think old exams are, both for tailoring your study right from the beginning of the semester and for preparing for the exam the week before. Two questions remain: How do you find old exams? Is it right to use them?

I've spoken to many instructors on the question of old exams. Most agree that if an instructor grades an exam and gives it back to the student, it becomes that student's property. What the student does with it or who it's given to is the student's business. Handing exams back to students means it is the instructor's responsibility to write new exams—or run the risk of having students do well only because they know the questions in advance.

Some instructors place old exams on file in the school library for access by all students; others keep files in their offices and allow students to look over old exams under supervision. Still others specifically prohibit the use of old exams in studying, and at some colleges such use of old exams is a violation of the school's honor code. Unless there *is* such a prohibition, I see nothing wrong with using old exams to study.

How do you go about finding old exams? If old exams are not readily available, they can usually be obtained from students who have taken the same class from the same professor. Fraternity brothers and sorority sisters are often excellent sources for this material. I never belonged to such an organization. I always just asked around to find out who had taken the class recently, and rarely did I have any problems finding old exams. The only rule associated with this kind of help is the obligation to offer the same assistance to your classmates when you can.

That brings up another question of ethics. Is it fair for some students to have access to old exams while their classmates do not? In fact, everyone has access if they're willing to look. If I'm asked by fellow students, I make the exams I have available. And I don't worry too much about the advantage this gives other students. Even when old exams are readily available, many students don't take the time to copy or study them. Just having, or having access to, an old exam doesn't guarantee you a better grade. You have to know how to incorporate it into your whole study scheme.

SUMMARY

If you use the study methods I've outlined in this book, you will be way ahead of your classmates by exam time, but there are some things you can do during the last week to increase this distance.

◆ Keep going to class, and—unless you've been told it will not be on the exam—spend 70 percent of your study time mastering the material presented during the final week before the exam.
◆ Spend the other 30 percent of your study time doing the following:

1. Review your original, noncondensed lecture notes at least once.
2. Review all old homework assignments.
3. Review all available old exams.
4. Look over any assigned reading material.
5. Early in the last week before the exam, ask the instructor any questions you haven't been able to answer on your own.
6. Don't spend a disproportionate amount of time studying material you already know: concentrate on what you don't know.
7. Attend all practice, review, or question sessions.
8. Take off the night, or even the afternoon, before the exam and relax.

YOU CAN DO IT!

Okay, be honest. How many times have you felt really well prepared as you sat down to begin an exam? How many times have you crammed? How many times have you pulled an all-nighter? What were the results of your efforts?

Now, how many times have you felt so well prepared the week before an exam that you didn't have to cram? What were the results of your efforts on that exam?

Are you ready to take the pledge? Repeat after me: *No more cramming!*

13

No Man—or Woman— Is an Island Until It's Time for an Exam

Okay. You've gone to all your classes, you've taken the time to develop a thorough understanding of the lecture and textbook material, and you've worked hard on your homework. But if you don't do well on the exam, most of your effort will have been wasted. In this chapter, I'll provide general tips for test taking and specific strategies for approaching some of the major types of exams given in college.

I'm making up statistics here, but I'm basing it on experience: No matter how well you have prepared for an exam, 15–20 percent of your test grade will depend on specific exam-taking skills. That means if you know the material well enough to get a 95, but you aren't good at taking tests, you may get only a 75—a C instead of an A! On multiple-choice ("multiple-guess," as some of my classmates call them) exams, your ability to eliminate answers effectively can make up for your lack of preparation—and panic and confusion can ruin hours of preparation. On an essay exam, an inability to think or express yourself under pressure will also bring your grade down. Many people do all the right work in preparation for an exam but have no specific approach to taking the exam. Don't let that be you.

EXAM ENVIRONMENT AND EMOTIONAL STRESS

Here's the scene: You're in your seat on exam day. The instructor looks like a state police officer, standing behind reflective sunglasses, pounding a billy club into an open palm. Your own palms are dripping sweat, and you're sure you are the only person in the room having this hallucination.

In fact, almost everyone in the room is as nervous as you are. Rising adrenaline levels cause your hands to shake, your stomach to churn, and your head to muddle. Under stressful circumstances, even the simplest things—speaking clearly or picking up a pencil and writing—may be difficult. This fight-or-flight response to frightening situations is biological; the production of adrenaline helps guarantee that you'll have the strength to run away from a threatening situation or to stand and fight.

There's not much need for physical strength in an exam, but the same adrenaline rush that makes you so shaky also helps you work hard until the exam is over, and you can use that anxiety-produced energy to your advantage. Knowing that this initial rush of adrenaline will make you shaky for the first ten–fifteen minutes is important in developing your test strategy.

EXAM-TAKING STRATEGIES

First Pass: Read the Whole Exam

Don't pick the hardest question on an exam to answer first, while you're still shaking so hard you can hardly hold your pencil. You'll calm down after ten or fifteen minutes; use that time to read through the test completely. On this pass, answer only the questions whose answers are immediately obvious to you, and place a mark next to those that appear more difficult. Make sure you go all the way through the test on this pass, answering the easy questions and marking the hard ones.

Don't allow yourself to get frustrated or hung up on any one problem in this first pass. Concentrate on what you know while your adrenaline is pumping because this takes the least amount of thinking at a time when you are not thinking clearly. *Do* pay attention to the questions that have the highest point value. You don't need to start working on them yet—unless they fit your definition of easy questions—but realize they're there, and get a grip on what they're about. Your brain may start searching for answers before you ask it to. Don't panic if some questions seem really tough; remember, your memory is like a well that requires a certain amount of priming before the water begins to flow. Just because you don't see the answer immediately doesn't mean that you're never going to.

Keep your eyes open for bits of information in one exam question that allow you to answer other questions. For example, a question on planet names may remind you of some bit of knowledge about the solar system that will help you answer another question. You may even find answers, or strong clues to answers, in other questions. I find that this occurs on many exams, particularly on long multiple-choice exams; and you can really help your score just by being alert.

Second Pass: Answer Questions of Highest Value First

After the first pass, you'll find that you have calmed down considerably. You're feeling good about having answered some questions, and you're ready to work on the problems that require more thought. Very often, you'll find that many problems that seemed difficult on the first pass are really quite easy. After many years of taking exams, I've come to believe that while I'm working on less difficult problems, my mind is subconsciously pondering the more difficult ones. Take it for what it's worth; it has served me well over the years.

I never dwell long on any one question that gives me problems until I have attempted every question. Then, when I'm sure I have calmed down from that initial adrenaline rush, I attempt to answer the problems of highest point value. This is a strategy I learned from Paul, who likes to order his questions according to their point value, choosing to do the "most expensive" ones first. Toward the end of an exam period, you may be tired and thinking less clearly than usual, or you may begin to panic as you see time running out. Once you've answered all the questions you find easy on the first pass, it's a good idea to answer the tougher (and more valuable) questions before that tiredness or panic sets in.

But don't carry this strategy too far; don't spend so much time on the high-point questions that you fail to answer others. Make sure you put something down for every question. Many times instructors will give partial credit to those who attempt a problem and get the wrong answer or don't finish it. Don't risk getting no credit at all for a question if there's even the slightest possibility of answering something reasonable.

Third Pass: Go Back Through the Whole Exam

Finally, after you have finished the second pass through the exam and have attempted to answer all the questions, use any additional time to go through the exam to reread and recalculate your answers. Quite often during this final pass, you'll find minor errors in grammar or arithmetic that could cost you important points.

Never leave an exam early. Often students brag about how quickly they finished. It's not who finishes first, it's who scores the highest. Use all the time available to recheck your answers—more than once, if you have that much time. If you're anything at all like me, you'll find something you missed every time you check. You've been thinking fast and writing fast, and it's easy to make errors under stressful conditions. I find that the questions I answered first (during the first fifteen minutes of the exam, when I'm still pretty nervous) are the ones that are most likely to need correcting. You may also find yourself suddenly remembering an additional important concept or groaning in exasperation (and relief) as you realize you answered No. 3 wrong—but you still have time to correct it.

Two warnings: Don't erase answers at the last minute when you don't have time to correct them; it's better to have a partially wrong answer than no answer at all. And don't change answers if you aren't sure that your second answer (or guess) is really better than your first.

TIME IS THE KEY

Few instructors (if any) give students an unlimited amount of time to take an exam. In fact, it's very common for the time allotted to be so deliberately limited that the majority of students will not be able to complete every question—let alone make all the passes just described. But the three-pass system lets you use the available time wisely. Remember, answer the obvious and easy questions first (which prevents you from losing points on material you know), attack the highest-value questions next, and—if you have the time—go through the whole exam a third time.

Often time is used, rather than tricky questions, to separate students according to their knowledge of the material. The theory is that a student who knows the exam material inside out (and who therefore deserves an A) should be able to finish the exam with just enough time to check over answers once. Those who are less familiar with the material will have to think more about each question and will therefore have more trouble finishing the exam in the time allotted.

This method of grading puts students who do not perform well under stress at a real disadvantage. Two students who are equally familiar with the material may act differently under the stress of an exam—and thus get very different grades.

If you use the constant-review methods stressed in this book, it will really pay off during a limited-time exam. While others are pondering theories and working through problems, you're racking up valuable points. It is also very important that you stick to your exam-taking strategies even when the clock is ticking and the pressure is on. By knowing the material inside out, and by knowing how to attack exams, even when time is limited, you'll become one of the students who *can* work well under stress.

The types and combinations of questions that could appear on an exam are endless, but my general advice is to allot amounts of time that seem appropriate for the number of points each question is worth. Never, never, never get hung up and spend a disproportionate amount of time on any one question until you have attempted them all and have done the easiest. What's a disproportionate amount of time? As you gain more experience in taking exams, you'll learn to gauge the amount of time you can afford to spend on various types of questions. Sometimes it's simple. For example, if you have four 25-point essay questions to answer in an hour, you'd better not spend more than ten minutes on each until you've had a chance to tackle them all; use the remaining time for the questions that need more work. If you have fifty multiple-choice questions, plan to spend less than a minute on each on the first pass.

A special bonus that comes with being well prepared: For many people, the knowledge that they have done their very best allows them to be quite relaxed during an exam. Who's going to feel better: the student who has covered absolutely every bit of material, or the student who never read the textbook assignments and attended only half the lectures? If you know you're very well prepared and you still feel you're doing poorly on an exam, take consolation in the idea that all those students who *aren't* prepared must be totally bombing it.

TYPES OF EXAM QUESTIONS

The three-pass test-taking strategy can be applied to almost any type of exam—from multiple-choice to essay exams—but special considerations may improve your performance on each.

Multiple-Choice Exams

I recommend the following procedure for multiple-choice tests: Read each question through once, making a mark to the right of any answer (*a, b, c,* or *d*) that you determine to be *in*correct. This is an excellent time-saving device. It allows you to narrow the choices down to one, two, or three answers, from which you choose more easily. The marks to the right of the incorrect answers serve as a reminder that those are wrong and do not need to be read again. On this first pass through a multiple-choice exam, don't forget to put a question mark next to any question you feel unsure about so you can go back and check this problem again on your second pass. When a multiple-choice question requires a mathematical calculation, you can often choose the correct answer after a quick estimate. The next section provides details about how to do this.

ATTACKING MULTIPLE-CHOICE EXAMS

Let's take a look at my multiple-choice-exam marking system. The first time through, put a question mark to the left of any question you need more time to consider. To narrow your choices, put a check to the right of any answer you're sure is *not* correct.

Sample Question:

Indiana
a. was the forty-ninth state to join the Union. ✓
b. is in the midwestern United States.
c. has a city named Cloverdale as its capital. ✓
d. is considered to be a mountainous state. ✓
e. shares borders with Ohio, Illinois, and Kansas.

Only the most clueless of students would select a, c, or d as the correct answer, so we mark those off on the first pass. Now, on the next pass you need to answer the question but you don't need to bother reading *a, c,* and *d* again; you already know they're wrong, and you don't have to waste time on them. On this pass, concentrate your efforts on choosing between *b* and *e*. If you have no idea, you'll still have a 50–50 chance of selecting the correct answer. If you've been studying hard, you'll be sure to get it right. Circle the letter corresponding to the correct answer to save time when you're checking answers and to record what you thought the correct answer was in case you have to re-mark your Scan Tron sheet.

Multiple-choice exams are usually given because they are an easy way for an instructor to grade a large number of exams in a short period of time. However, you should be aware of several potentially serious pitfalls in this exam format.

1. When you have made an answer selection for a particular question, you have to record it on a Scan Tron sheet. Because the Scan Tron sheet has a multitude of little round bubbles placed very close together, it is very easy to mark a bubble in the wrong row (for example, mark your answer for No. 10 in space No. 11). This mistake is compounded with each subsequent answer you mark on the

Scan Tron. If you make such an error early in the exam, it can be fatal. What's the easiest way to avoid this? Never leave a question on a multiple-choice exam unanswered, even if you don't have a clue and intend to attempt it again on your second pass. By always putting something down, you help ensure you will keep your subsequent answers in the right order.

2. It's easy to get confused about what you thought the right answer was on the first or second pass, especially if you've marked the Scan Tron sheet incorrectly or look at the wrong spot when you're double-checking answers. When you select your answer for a particular question, circle the letter corresponding to that answer (*a, b, c,* and so on) on your exam sheet next to the corresponding question in addition to marking the Scan Tron answer sheet. This can be very helpful when you check your answers on a subsequent pass, and it saves valuable time if you get your Scan Tron sheet out of order and have to change it all at the last minute. In classes where the question sheet is collected with the Scan Tron sheet, you may be able to convince an instructor to change your grade based on those answers instead of the incorrectly marked Scan Tron if you do goof up. (But don't count on it!)

3. You can really waste time on a multiple-choice exam by agonizing over tough or confusing questions. If you read through the answer choices for a given question and decide that *a* and *e* could not possibly be right but you just can't decide between *b, c,* and *d,* I suggest you make your most educated guess—or even a totally *un*educated guess. Don't keep going back and wasting time second- and third-guessing yourself and changing your answer. Chances are good that your first hunch on these complicated questions is best. Don't run the risk of getting your answers mixed up and out of order by changing them. If, on the other hand, the correct answer suddenly becomes obvious to you and you are now *sure* you've selected the wrong answer, then by all means go back and change it.

4. It's easy to read too much into multiple-choice questions. A clever (some say diabolical) teacher will include questions that might be interpreted a number of ways, depending on the answers provided. In situations like this, keep it simple. If you feel yourself being seduced by a complicated read on a particular question, go back and read it more carefully, looking for the simplest interpretation. Don't overanalyze the question, and don't hesitate to ask the instructor for clarification if you need it. Put down what you think is the best answer, and go on with the rest of the test. Later, during your recheck, see if you still agree with that answer.

5. It's common for an instructor to include at least one choice that is

very close to being correct except for some small detail. You'll often see this when you read through the answer choices for the first time and mark the ones you know are wrong; when you finish, you're left with two very similar answers. Read them closely: One is the correct answer, and the other is a plant used to separate students who know the material really well from those who just kind of know it.

6. It only takes one little word in a question to change its entire meaning. I call these words "qualifiers," or negatives. If you're not looking for them, they can be disastrous. I'll use two oversimplified multiple-choice questions to illustrate my point.

1. Which names of the following months do not start with the letter *J*?
   a. January
   b. June
   c. July
   d. April
   e. a, b, and c
2. The following animals are all mammals except
   a. kangaroos
   b. koalas
   c. wallabies
   d. kiwis
   e. a, b, and c

It's easy to read a question like No. 1 and miss the negative ("do not"), especially under the stress of an exam. If you make this mistake, you'll be giving the wrong answer (*e*) simply because you overlooked two small but critical words. A similar mistake could be made in No. 2. If you overlook the word "except," you again might choose the wrong answer (*e*). Always look for one or two words in a question that can cause you to choose the wrong answer; some other examples of these words are "could," "always," "never," "may be," "usually," and "sometimes." I make it a point to circle these words in a question to remind me that they are there, and I pause for a second and ask myself what exactly the question is asking. (By the way, the correct answer for both questions is *d*).

Math Exams

Whenever you try to answer questions requiring mathematical calculations, you should know the approximate size of the answer you are seeking. Calculators can malfunction, or your fingers can punch the wrong buttons during the stress of an exam. Determine the approximate size of the answer and whether it is positive or negative by using this method: Round numbers to something simple to multiply or divide in your head or very quickly on scratch paper. For example, if you're asked to multiply 596 by 421, round the first number up and the second number down.

$$600 \times 400 = 240,000.$$

This gets you close to the actual answer: 250,916.

The rule of thumb with multiplication is this: If both numbers are rounded down, your estimate will be low; if both are rounded up, the estimate will be high. When dividing, you'll get the most useful results if you round the numerator and the denominator both up or both down. For example,

$$596/287 = 2.1.$$

If you round both numbers up, you get

$$600/300 = 2.0.$$

Sometimes the estimates are close enough to choose the right answer on a multiple-choice exam without using a calculator to get the exact answer. This can save you some valuable time.

Nothing I have learned in the past eight years in college has been of more use than a mathematical technique called "dimensional analysis," or "flip-flops." While math teachers and tutors can give you lots of tricks and shortcuts, this is such a useful technique that I want to teach it to you here. Dimensional analysis is a very useful and powerful tool that uses ratios to make conversions, and you can use it in real life as well as in college classes. Here's an example:

Question: How many hours is 5,457 seconds?

To start to answer a question like this, you must ask yourself, What do I *want?* and What do I *have?* What you *want* is an answer in hours, and what you *have* is the time in seconds.

Let's say you don't know how many seconds there are in an hour, but you do know how many seconds there are in a minute and how many minutes there are in an hour. With flip-flops, you set up ratios that are equal to one.

$$1 \text{ minute} = 60 \text{ seconds}$$

therefore $\dfrac{1 \text{ minute}}{60 \text{ seconds}} = 1$, and $\dfrac{60 \text{ seconds}}{1 \text{ minute}} = 1$

$$1 \text{ hour} = 60 \text{ minutes}$$

therefore $\dfrac{1 \text{ hour}}{60 \text{ minutes}} = 1$, and $\dfrac{60 \text{ minutes}}{1 \text{ hour}} = 1$

These ratios can be used as conversion factors to get the answer you're looking for. They're called "flip-flops" because you can use them right side up or upside down.

Set up all the flip-flops in the equation so that units cancel. In the example above, you can convert to minutes from seconds and to hours from minutes. Whenever a particular unit of measurement (minutes, hours, feet, grams, and so on) appears both in the denominator and in the numerator anywhere in the equation, you can cross both out.

In this example, notice how all the units cancel except hours, which is what we want. This is what makes this technique so useful. If you can't cross out all the units of measurement except the one you want for the final answer, you've goofed somewhere and need to start again. Even with a string of eight or ten conversion factors, you can be confident you've set them up correctly if all the units cancel. In this example, multiplication gives us our answer: 1.5 hours.

Question: 5,457 seconds = how many hours?

Have   Want

$$5{,}457 \text{ seconds} \times \frac{1 \text{ minute}}{60 \text{ seconds}} \times \frac{1 \text{ hour}}{60 \text{ minutes}} = 1.5 \text{ hours}$$

Let's try one more example:

Question: 4.7×10^6 inches = how many miles?

Have   Want

$$4.7 \times 10^6 \text{ inches} \times \frac{1 \text{ foot}}{12 \text{ inches}} \times \frac{1 \text{ yard}}{3 \text{ feet}} \times \frac{1 \text{ mile}}{1{,}760 \text{ yds}} = 74.2 \text{ miles}$$

Notice how in both examples the units cancel out, leaving us with the desired units, i.e., hours in the first example and miles in the second example.

These mathematical shortcuts are useful, not only for math problems but also for chemistry and physics problems and even for simply figuring out how many ounces there are in a gallon.

As in all exams, don't be afraid to put something down on a math question even if it is just your best guess or a wild fling at an answer. This is a last resort after you've done your second pass. But never leave a question blank. Other students probably are having the same problem with that particular question, and this often leads the professor to be more generous or lenient when grading it. Also critical: Write down all the steps in a calculation as you perform them so that the instructor can see that you were on the right track. You may get partial credit even if your final answer is wrong or you run out of time before you reach a final answer. But if you don't put anything down, the teacher has no reason to be generous and you will automatically lose the points.

Essay Exams

Since the dawn of testing, students have dreaded essay questions on exams. Conquering your fear is half the battle here. If you really know the material, you ought to be able to write about it coherently. And with a few tips about how to attack essay questions, you'll be even more confident.

The method of answering essay questions that has always worked well for me is this: First, be sure you know what you're being asked. As in multiple-choice exams, misinterpreting the question can lead to real problems with the answer. Is the instructor asking you to *describe* something, to *compare* one thing with another, to *define* something, to *outline* the events leading up to something, to *explain* a process, to *list* the components of a theory? If there is real confusion over the intent of the question, ask the teacher for clarification.

The first sentence of your answer should let the instructor know what you think you're being asked; it should restate the question *as you understand it*. Sometimes, despite your best efforts to understand, it turns out that the instructor had a different direction in mind. Your restatement of the question lets the instructor see why you answered the question the way you did. If you can answer your interpretation of the question appropriately, the instructor may grade it more leniently.

Second, don't get caught up in trying to answer the whole question all at once. Present and deal with one idea at a time. Use the margin or the back of the exam paper to make a brief list of ideas associated with the topic of the question. If you run out of time before you can finish an essay question, an instructor may give partial credit for this list of supporting ideas.

After you've stated your understanding of the question, state your thesis. A "thesis" is your argument or answer summarized in one or two sentences, and it sets the direction for your essay. It can often be combined with your interpretation of the question; see my example below. The subsequent material presented in the body of your essay should be directed at supporting this thesis.

Third, check your list of associated ideas and select those that really help to answer the question. Order them logically, and flesh them out. Weave in the additional facts you believe will support your answer. Don't try to be flowery, and resist the temptation to write down everything you know about the subject; use only those facts and ideas that answer the question. Instructors always recognize padding and are usually irritated by it, and the last thing you want to do is irritate the person grading your exam.

After you've presented all the pertinent facts to support your thesis, summarize your thesis and supporting material in a short, comprehensive paragraph. (If you've run out of time, this step can be omitted.) In this step, you may also want to draw conclusions from your other statements.

Let's use, as an example, an essay question that you might get in a course using this book as a text. This sample question will illustrate my approach to essay exams.

Essay sample question: What is the general approach to taking exams that John Stowers recommends? Describe its components, and explain its benefits.

First, think about what the instructor is asking. The question mentions no specific type of exam, so steer clear of details about essay, multiple-choice, or math exams. What the instructor is looking for here is an overall approach. Make a list of whatever you remember from that section of the chapter. Such a list might look like this:

1. Expect adrenaline and nervousness.
2. Read whole exam.
3. Answer easy questions.
4. Go through again and try all.

5. *Answer high-value questions first.*
6. *Proofread exam and check answers.*
7. *Never leave early.*
8. *Never leave questions unanswered.*

Before answering the question, restate it, showing what you believe it to be asking. Then answer it briefly. At this point, you might suddenly panic and think, "Oh, no—what if it's really asking how to *study* for exams? I'm sunk!" By restating your interpretation of the question here, you let the instructor know why you're answering the way you are.

John Stowers's general approach to taking exams is summarized in his description of the three-pass method.

Next, expand your list of supporting ideas into support for this introductory statement and to answer the "describe" and "explain benefits" sections of the question.

According to this strategy, the student should first read the entire exam, answering easy questions and marking those he needs to come back to later. This lets the student use up some of the nervous energy caused by the surge of adrenaline test-takers feel and gives him some idea of what lies ahead so his brain can begin searching for answers. During the second pass of this strategy, every question should be attempted; and Stowers emphasizes that you should never leave any questions without answers because you might be able to get at least partial credit if you answer something. Stowers also recommends that you answer the questions that are worth the most points first so that if you run out of time, you at least have done some high-point questions. On this second pass, Stowers points out, you may find questions you can answer because of something you read or thought about in another question somewhere else on the exam. On the third pass, Stowers recommends, you should check all your answers and proofread for spelling and grammatical errors. On an exam requiring calculations, you should recalculate answers to avoid arithmetic errors costing you points.

Finally, summarize your answer.

John Stowers's three-pass approach to taking exams is a strategy that allows students to minimize errors caused by nervousness, utilize time effectively, and maximize their chances of getting a good grade.

I'm not claiming that this is the world's greatest answer to this question, but I think it gives you an idea of how to approach essay exams. The first sentence shows how you plan to answer the question. Suppose you had actually thought the instructor meant studying for as opposed to taking an exam? Your first sentence would reflect this difference; it might have been something like, "John Stowers's study method of three-back one-ahead ensures that the week before an exam, you won't be cramming." Making the list of related issues right away reminds you of all the things you need to include in the answer and lets you think about how to order those ideas. The concluding paragraph ties things together.

Always proofread your essay, first for content and then for grammar and spelling. This second point is often overlooked but can be very important. While most non-English classes do not grade grammar and spelling directly, anything that makes it difficult for instructors to read essays may lower your grade. Such errors can even lead to a misinterpretation of your answer. Keep in mind that your essay is but one of countless others that your instructor must read; anything you can do to make your essay stand out from the others will help your grade.

Matching, True-or-False, and Short-Answer Questions

Most students have taken plenty of matching, true-or-false, and short-answer exams by the time they get to college, so I'm not going to spend a lot of time discussing them. You can use the three-pass strategy on any kind of exam, including these. A few other comments might be helpful.

1. When matching and true-or-false questions are to be answered on a Scan Tron sheet, all my cautions about using these (see the section on multiple-choice questions) apply.
2. True-or-false questions, like multiple-choice questions, can trip you up because of just one or two little words. Be sure you understand what the statement says before you decide whether it's true or

false. Watch especially for words such as "not," "never," "usually," "may be," and "always."

3. Short-answer questions usually require just what they say: *short answers.* This is not the time to develop an essay or ramble aimlessly. Give a brief but complete definition of a term or a succinct answer to a question. If you're worried that the instructor may be looking for more than the question clearly asks, ask something like this: Do you want us to describe the details of the plot of *Moby Dick* or just give a one-sentence synopsis?

4. Matching questions usually lend themselves nicely to an elimination strategy: First match up everything you're sure about, and then tackle the questions you feel capable of guessing about. By the time you've taken those two steps, there should be very few left, and you'll have a reasonable chance of making the right matches for them.

Lab Practicals: A Special Challenge

College may be the first time you encounter laboratory exams, often called "lab practicals." These exams require you to perform tasks beyond simply reading questions and writing answers. You may have to look at pickled animal specimens or microscope slides and identify various features. You may have to create a computer program to solve a problem. You may have to identify an unknown substance in a chemistry lab.

These exams vary so much, and are such a surprise to students who have never taken one, that I urge you to find out as much as you can about them before exam time. It's not at all unusual for a student who has done well on written exams to really flop on the practical, simply because of a lack of experience. Ask the instructor what will be required of you. Ask other students about their experiences with lab exams. Go to all the review sessions. If the instructor doesn't offer one, request a practice exam. Even a small sample of what the real thing will be like will help you prepare.

SUMMARY

☆ Use my three-pass method for attacking exams: (1) Spend ten–fifteen minutes reading through the whole exam and answering the easy questions, (2) go through it again, answering the questions with the highest point value first, and (3) if you have time, make a third pass through the exam to check your answers.

☆ Tailor your exam-taking strategy to the specific type of exam.

☆ Don't try to read too much into exam questions; keep your interpretations simple and direct. When you are confused, ask for clarification.

☆ *Never* leave a question unanswered. Put *something* down for every question, especially multiple-choice questions. Even if you don't have a clue as to the real answer, make an effort. If nothing else, the teacher may give you credit for effort—or for entertainment.

☆ Watch for the special pitfalls of multiple-choice exams, especially when Scan Tron sheets are used.

☆ Use dimensional analysis (flip-flops) to answer questions requiring conversion from one unit of measurement to another.

☆ Use estimates to check your answers to math questions.

☆ Approach essay exams as follows: Outline the main points you wish to cover, and then order them logically. Your first paragraph should contain a restatement of the question and your thesis. Support your thesis with the logically ordered points. Conclude with a complete but brief summary of these points. Keep your essay direct and to the point. Proofread the whole essay.

If you use the study methods presented in this book, you will know the exam material well; and if you use the exam methods, you will provide good, clear answers to questions and finish on time, all of which will maximize your score. At test time, straight-A students have already been testing themselves for weeks. So relax. And start answering questions.

YOU CAN DO IT!

Think about your most recent exam. Let's assess your test-taking abilities.

Did you read over the whole exam quickly?

Did you answer the easiest questions first?

Did you attack the questions with the highest point value next?

Did you check over your answers and proofread your essay?

Did you have time to finish the exam?

Did you leave the exam early?

Did you lose points for questions you could have answered if you'd had more time?

Did you lose points for questions you knew how to answer but made silly mistakes on?

Were you nervous during the exam?

Do you think nervousness prevented you from doing as well as you could have?

Did you feel well-prepared when the exam began?

14

Going to School
Part-Time

With growing economic hardship and the changing dynamics of the family, students in the 1990s are faced with many challenges, not the least of which is the financial burden of supporting themselves while trying to brighten their futures by getting a college education. At times, this can be a Catch 22: If you're self-supporting and have to work, it's difficult to attend school full-time; and if you attend school full-time and try to improve your future opportunities, it's difficult to support yourself.

Students in ever increasing numbers are finding it more realistic to attend college part-time while supplementing their incomes by working full-time or part-time. In fact, in 1990, 41 percent of all college students—approximately 5 million—attended only part-time, and two-thirds of these were employed. I did this myself for a few semesters, and in this chapter I'll try to help you avoid some of the problems I faced should you decide to go this route.

WHAT'S PART-TIME?

The U.S. Department of Education defines a part-time college student as someone who is taking less than 75 percent of a full-time course load. A distinction is also made between a part-time student and a half-time student. While these numbers may vary one or two units from college to college, in general, a half-time student is one who is taking fewer than 6 units, and a part-time student is one who is taking 6–11 units. This distinction can affect the federal loans, grants, and scholarships available to part-time students; I'll say more about that in Special Topics in the back of the book, where I provide some general information about financial aid.

WHY ATTEND PART-TIME?

There are many reasons for attending college part-time. Some students know they want further education but are not quite sure which area of study is right for them; attending part-time allows them to sample classes in possible areas of interest while keeping their options open. If your application was rejected by the college you really wanted to attend, you can still attend part-time. And sometimes establishing a good grade record there on a part-time basis can help your next application. Another benefit of attending part-time is that older students often do better in college than those just out of high school, and while you're taking a few courses, you're gaining in maturity as well as getting some college experience. But finances are the most common reason for part-time attendance, as shown by a study done by the American Council on Education.

GOAL SETTING FOR THE PART-TIME STUDENT

Ever heard the expression jack-of-all-trades, master of none? This can be a serious problem for the part-time student, but well-defined goals can help you avoid the problem.

Let me explain. Life holds many challenges for part-time students. Not only do they have to attend class and study, but many—perhaps most—have to work. Many also have families to support and obligations other than school. In fact, for the part-time student, college performance often is forced to take a backseat. Unfortunately, sometimes spreading your time among too many things can prevent you from mastering any one of them or from achieving your goals.

Set realistic goals. Thinking out goals for both your education and your personal life can help you avoid a lot of heartache and frustration. If your goal is to get straight A's and you're taking a full load at college, working full-time, and are involved in other time-consuming activities, it's only a matter of time before something gives. If you have to work full-time, and you need to get A's in your classes, cut your school load back or plan to give up everything else in your life for the semester. This advice may sound obvious, but often part-time students are ambitious people, and sometimes they set unrealistic goals for themselves.

With careful planning, overextending yourself can be prevented. Once you have defined your academic goals, develop a plan that allows you to realize them.

DEVISING THE PLAN

Let's say your goal is to get an undergraduate degree and to get straight A's along the way. For financial or other important reasons, you decide to work full-time and go to school part-time. The plan you develop must account for your goals, your personal and school obligations, and the time you have available. Your plan should allow you to make the most effective use of your limited time.

Sample Plan: Full-Time Employment

You work eight hours a day and you need to get straight A's in college. How many credit hours (units) can you take and still work and get the grades you need? Let's look at where your time is spent each day and devise a plan.

Eight hours of your day is spent at work. Adequate sleep helps reduce the stress of working and going to school. We'll budget eight hours a night for you. Another five hours a day goes to necessary tasks such as eating, personal hygiene, and commuting. If we subtract all this time from twenty-four hours, we're left with three hours a day to put into education. (This doesn't include additional time on the weekend that can be used for catching up or studying for a big exam.)

These numbers are only rough estimates and are going to vary from person to person. But this is how you might go about planning your own schedule, using numbers that reflect your needs and lifestyle. Do you sing in the church choir? Subtract the two hours you spend in rehearsal Thursday nights. Coach your daughter's soccer team? Subtract that time, too.

Now that you know how much time you'll have available, how do you know how much time you'll need? A rough rule of thumb used on college campuses across the country is that for every hour of in-class time, you should allot at least two hours for studying. Of course, this is a crude estimate that will vary from class to class, college to college, and student to student. But it's a good place to start in developing your plan.

Approximately how many credit hours per semester could you take without overextending yourself? Let's use the estimate of two hours out of class for every hour in. If you have three hours each day you can devote to education, you have a total of fifteen hours during the work-week. Now, let's see how it would work if you were to take six semester units (credit hours). Six hours a week of in-class is going to require approximately twelve hours of studying outside of class; that's a total of eighteen hours spent each week pursuing your education.

"Wait!" you say, "the sample forty-hour workweek only allowed me fifteen hours!" But we didn't figure in any weekend time. This was intentional because it goes back to my original rule: Don't overextend yourself! Now we can use the weekend to make up the additional three hours a week we need for studying, but you really shouldn't count on these weekend hours when you're doing your original plan. If you take six credit hours, we see now, you'll have time on the weekend to study for that big exam or to catch up on personal chores you didn't get to during the week.

What if you take nine units instead of six, however? You'd have to spend a total of twenty-seven hours a week either in class or studying. If you have fifteen hours during the week budgeted for school, you're left with about twelve hours to make up for on the weekend. In my opinion, this is overextending yourself. Not only is it a tough schedule but it's probably not an effective route to good grades. Marathon cram sessions on the weekends are not nearly as effective as studying in smaller intervals throughout the week.

This example should give you an idea of how to develop a schedule that fits your personal needs. The estimate that one hour of class requires two hours of study is only a place to start. Some classes, and for that matter some students, require more time; others require less. I also assumed that you're striving for A's. Obviously, if your goal is to get B's, you may not have to work as hard and may be able to take a heavier class load.

AVOID THE PART-TIME PITFALLS

Ever played one of those video games where you've forded a river full of deadly piranha, crawled through a dark cave full of killer vampire bats, fought off an army of troll people, and—just when you're about to rescue the princess—fallen through a deadly trapdoor and had to start all over again? College can be like that at times, especially for part-time students. Like those frustrating video games, college also can hold many pitfalls. Recognizing them can save you lots of trouble and ease your path to straight A's.

Being Out of the Loop

Probably the biggest pitfall of the part-time student is that of being out of the loop—the information loop, that is. Because part-time students spend less time on campus and often take their classes in the evening, they may miss out on school services and events. They also may not get information about important deadlines or class scheduling and curriculum changes.

What can you do to overcome this problem? I suggest you take the time to develop a good relationship with your academic adviser. You may have to make a special effort to meet with your adviser, but such meetings could go a long way toward helping you graduate. As a part-time student, you may also have more of a problem networking than do your full-time counterparts, but networking is even more important for you than for them. Form relationships with other students (see Chapter 6) for the purpose of sharing information about classes and instructors and for sharing old exams. It's probably most useful to make friends with full-time students because they can provide you with the kind of information that's available only to students who are on campus all day. The additional time you may need to devote to forming these relationships will pay big dividends in the form of higher grades. Other suggestions for avoiding the out-of-the-loop problem include reading the student newspaper frequently, listening to a campus radio station, and paying attention to bulletin board notices.

Being a part-time student may technically entitle you to the same opportunities and services as full-time students: counseling centers, writing centers, financial aid offices, and the like. But many of these services can be accessed only during regular business hours or on a very limited basis in the evening. This can be a real problem for students who are working during the day and attending evening classes. You may have to make special arrangements at work to use such services. If you're planning to take time off work, call ahead and make appointments at each center or office you need to visit. Explain that you work full-time and need to be sure you'll be able to accomplish your purpose when you reach the office.

Finding the Classes You Need

Part-time students often have difficulty finding the classes they need during the limited hours they have available for taking them. If you're faced with this problem, there are several things you can try.

1. Check to see if the class you want to take might be offered the following semester at a time that better fits your work schedule.
2. Check to see if there is another class that might fulfill the same requirement and is offered at a more convenient time.
3. Find out whether there's any possibility of completing the course requirements on an independent study basis. This stands the best chance of success if the instructor is someone whose class you have attended previously, who knows that you're a good student, and who trusts that you'll do the work.
4. Many colleges have classes on videotape and on cable TV channels; see if this is a possibility at your school.
5. See if you can take a similar course at another school, perhaps at a community or technical college. Prior approval is essential if you decide to go this route.
6. Investigate "clepping out" of some requirements; that is, taking CLEP exams to obtain credit for material you already know, either from high school or because you've taught it to yourself.

IT'S NOT ALL BAD

Being a part-time student has some advantages. As a part-time student, you can make the most of your education. While full-time students are juggling many different classes, part-time students have the opportunity to concentrate their time and effort into two or three specific courses. Being a part-time student can also provide you with valuable opportunities to spend more time on nonschool activities. This can be very important to the student who lists "living a balanced life" as one of his personal and educational goals.

SUMMARY

One of the most obvious solutions to the problem of not having enough money to go to college is to work part-time or full-time and go to school part-time. Getting through college on a part-time basis presents special challenges, and in this chapter I have provided some tips for meeting those challenges.

☆ Set educational goals, and use these goals to devise a plan for getting through college.

☆ Don't overextend yourself!

☆ Use my sample plan to decide on the number of credit hours to take in one semester.

☆ Take steps to compensate for being out of the information loop: Stay in touch with your academic adviser, make friends with your classmates, and read the student newspaper.

☆ Be aware that you may have trouble scheduling required classes, and be creative in overcoming that difficulty.

YOU CAN DO IT!

Are you considering attending college on a part-time basis? Let's calculate how many credit hours you should take. Answer these questions to help you arrive at a reasonable schedule.

How many hours does your job take each day?

How many hours do you spend sleeping each day?

How many hours each day do you spend on other activities? (Include meals; church, social, or volunteer activities; personal hygiene; and family obligations. It may help to try to keep track of your activities for a week.)

Now, add these three numbers, subtract this total from twenty-four hours, and multiply by five to see how many hours during the workweek you can devote to education.

Finally, use the estimate of two hours out of class for each hour in class to see how many credits you can take.

15

Student Stress

You've just bought a book entitled *Straight A's: If I Can Do It, So Can You.* You're in college, or about to go, and you're hoping to do well. You have drive, you have determination—and you have stress.

As an undergraduate student, you can be under more stress than at any other time in your educational career. Unfortunately, you may also have little support. One of the keys to getting straight A's in college is learning how to recognize and manage stress. In this chapter, I'll tell you how to do that.

DO YOU KNOW STRESS WHEN YOU SEE IT?

Stress can come in all shapes and sizes. Some stress is placed on us by others, and some we place on ourselves. Some stress is from good things and some from bad. Some you can change, and some you can't. Some people say they work better under stress; some break down. Whatever the source and whatever the result, chronic stress is not healthy.

How do you know when you're stressed out? On the surface, this seems like a ridiculous question. Obviously, if your wife, boyfriend, or significant other just left you, you're stressed. If your rent is due next week and the engine just fell out of your car, you're stressed. If you have a big exam coming up, you're probably stressed—although, if you're following the strategy laid out in this book, you're not as stressed as you could be!

But what if you just hit the lottery for a cool million? What if you just met the significant other of your dreams? What if you just got straight A's for the third semester in a row? Are you stressed? Chances are you wouldn't recognize it if you were.

How can you recognize stress in your life when it's not so obvious? Be on the lookout for changes in your eating and sleeping habits. Are you gaining or losing weight? Are you more irritable than usual? Has it been a couple of weeks or more since you last exercised or did something enjoyable just for yourself? Are the people close to you in your life saying that you "just haven't been yourself lately"? Have you had more than your share of colds, infections, and flu bugs? If you answer yes to any one of these questions, chances are good that you're stressed.

THE STUDENT STRESS CYCLE

Stress for students can run in cycles. You'll probably never see the following cycle described in a psychology textbook or magazine, but you probably will see it in yourself or your friends. Recognizing where you are in this stress cycle can be the first and most important step in breaking the cycle.

Let's start the cycle at the beginning of a new semester or school year. You see an end coming to all the free time you had over summer vacation or spring break. Last week you waited in long lines to register for classes or buy books, and now you're thrown into classes full of strange faces. A semester of work lies ahead of you. To adapt to this new demand, you decide to set priorities and cut back on some of your less important—but enjoyable—activities. For most students this is mild stress.

As the semester rolls on and midterm exams arrive, your level of stress jumps. You realize that there just isn't enough time in the day and you need those A's, so you decide that for the rest of the semester you're going to give up the exercise program that is so important to you. After all, you reason, it's only for the rest of the semester; you can get back in shape later. Big mistake! This was an important source of stress release for you, and now you're probably experiencing medium stress.

You now head downhill quickly. You resent the fact that you had to give up your exercise program, you begin to skip meals, and you're not sleeping well. This is chronic stress, *and it's not healthy!*

Now final exams are on the way. All those papers and homework assignments you haven't even started are due next week. Your time and energy are stretched to the max, but you think you'll just make it. Oh, no! On your way to school today the engine in your car blew up. You miss the entire day of classes, and you don't know where you're going to get the money to fix your car. It's hopeless. You break down. This is what I call the "collapse phase" of the stress cycle. Some students get sick right before or during exam week; others put it off until right after exams. But physical illness is a common symptom of this collapse phase.

During this phase, you decide that nothing is more important than your mental and physical health. How did you get so overextended? You reevaluate your personal and academic goals; you go back to your exercise program. Unfortunately, what with missed classes, lack of sleep, and a stress-induced inability to study or even pay attention during lectures, you don't do well on those final exams. But now you've learned your lesson, and you're going to make sure this doesn't happen again next semester.

PREVENTING AND MANAGING STRESS

Breaking the stress cycle can be difficult. Often it seems to feed on itself. Each semester, the obligations on your time and the predisposing factors repeat themselves while you're even *less* able to handle them than you were before because of your mounting anxiety about your poor grades and the courses you've failed to complete.

Instead of breaking the cycle, therefore, let's prevent it from getting started. If you are the student I described above, you are not following my advice about keeping up in classes, attending lectures, working on assignments ahead of time, and reviewing constantly to avoid the necessity of cramming before exams. You would find yourself far less vulnerable to stress if you applied the study methods presented in this book. One of my favorite sayings about my college experience is this: "When the going gets tough, the tough get organized." That's what this book is about—getting organized. It's the key to success in college, and an organized life is a less stressful one. Simply incorporating all my time-management and study methods into your academic life will go a long way toward preventing stress.

The next best prevention tip I can give you is about your attitude, and it goes back to Chapter 1, where I compared college to a game. Of course your education is important, but not at the cost of your physical or mental health. Experts on job stress recommend that people find work that for them is play; that is, that they really enjoy in an environment they feel comfortable in and with people they like. If you can think of college as a game you're playing—and should be enjoying—you should be able to reduce your stress levels significantly.

Even those who take life calmly for the most part sometimes experience stress, though. Here are several specific suggestions for managing or preventing stress as you work your way toward your college goals:

1. Play as hard as you work. (Notice that I didn't say "as *much*.") Every hard-working student needs a release, something not related to schoolwork. As I've already mentioned, aerobic exercise is useful for relieving stress; since there are only so many hours in a day, many people choose hobbies and stress relievers that incorporate some form of exercise, thereby killing two birds with one stone. Choose something that you can do at least every other day, something that involves concentration, and something that gives you satisfaction and allows for personal achievement.

2. Seek help. This can range from talking to friends about your problems to going to the campus counseling center, where trained psychologists can give you a new perspective on life. Depression and anxiety are common among college students; don't let them ruin— or end—your life. When you're feeling really stressed, get yourself to someone who can help: your minister, a friend, your parents, a physician, a counselor. If you feel suicidal, tell them; and if the first person you tell laughs it off, tell another person. Likewise, take it seriously if a friend tells you he or she is feeling really bad. Talking about suicide ("I feel like life isn't worth living," "No one would miss me if I were dead," "I may as well kill myself," "Killing myself would solve all my problems") is a call for help. Make sure you and your friends get the help you need.

3. Limit your involvement in extracurricular activities. College campuses are full of causes to commit yourself to and fun things to do. Some students want to raise money for a special interest, others want you to join their fraternity, and still others want you to join a petition drive to change something on campus. The one thing such activities have in common is that they take time away from your school and personal life—and they can cause a considerable amount of stress. Stay focused on your primary goals and your reasons for attending college.

4. Be aware of the importance of food and rest in combatting stress. A

healthy diet and enough sleep can help you cope with the demands of college life. Unfortunately, students often fall into a pattern of skipping meals or skimping on sleep to study and then feeling more stress because of inadequate rest and food. If you feel pressed for time, try reading and reviewing notes while you're eating, and read Chapter 10 again for other time-management tips. If you have sleep problems, consider seeing a counselor for tips on solving them.

5. Try to use stress to your advantage. Feeling nervous about the upcoming exam? Channel your nervousness into study instead of into eating brownies or watching TV. Are you awake in the middle of the night because of anxiety? Get out your calculus homework problems and attack them.

6. Reevaluate your academic goals periodically. Are you trying to accomplish too much too quickly? You may decide you need to drop one course to salvage the others. Don't be afraid to take such a step. It's better to admit defeat in one class than to struggle on and do poorly in all your classes. Maybe you need to take a semester off, or drop back to part-time status, or take some other steps to regain your mental and physical health.

7. Take time out each week to ask yourself a few basic questions: Am I happy? Am I doing what I want to do? Is this how I want to live my life? Is my stress level worth the goal I'm trying to reach? Don't wake up one day and realize you've been on the wrong track for years, or even weeks. Life is too short to waste.

8. Experiment with relaxation techniques, yoga, and meditation to control stress. Many good books on these subjects are available, and many campuses offer workshops or information at counseling centers on such methods of stress reduction.

9. Don't let alcohol or drugs ruin your chances of graduating. The temptation to relax and have fun at college via drugs or alcohol is great. I won't try to tell you it's *impossible* both to do well in college and to use drugs or alcohol. But I will tell you this: People with drug or alcohol problems often have serious academic problems, and the only way you can get to the point of having a drug or alcohol problem is by drinking or doing drugs. You know why casinos offer free drinks? Because the managers know that drunks have impaired judgment, and that means more money for the casino. You can't study, listen to lectures, or take exams effectively if you're tanked up. I don't want to preach, and I can't say an occasional good time is going to jeopardize your chances to get straight A's. But in general, substance abuse and good grades are incompatible.

SUMMARY

The best defense against stress is a good offense. Recognize the warning signs and the sources of stress in your life, and take steps to deal with them before they deal with you. Let's review my tips for alleviating stress.

☆ Learn to recognize it.

☆ Determining where you are in the student stress cycle is a good first step toward breaking the stress cycle.

☆ Apply the study methods presented in this book to help you organize your life and keep up to date in all your classes.

☆ Participate regularly in some sort of activity that releases stress, one that requires concentration and provides aerobic exercise.

☆ Seek help when you're feeling really stressed, anxious, or depressed.

☆ Avoid getting caught up in too many extracurricular activities.

☆ Get adequate rest, and eat a balanced diet.

☆ Use stress to your advantage when possible.

☆ Reevaluate your goals, and drop back if necessary.

☆ Assess your overall happiness frequently.

☆ Try various relaxation techniques to help manage stress.

☆ Don't let substance abuse ruin your academic career.

YOU CAN DO IT!

Managing stress is an achievable goal for most college students, but it takes some dedication. Take the quiz below to assess your current level of stress management.

From each of the following pairs of statements, check the one that best describes you.

_____ I get at least a couple of hours of sleep every night.

_____ I get six–eight hours of sleep every night.

_____ My meals are a reasonable balance of grains, vegetables, fruits, and meats or dairy products.

_____ My meals are a reasonable balance of grease, sugar, caffeine, and carbonates.

_____ I'm pretty much up to date in all my classes.

_____ If a miracle occurs, I may make it through most of my classes.

_____ The last time I exercised was in elementary school.

_____ The last time I exercised was during the past week.

_____ I know where I would go to get help if I felt stressed.

_____ If I felt stressed, I would keep it a big secret.

Chapter

16

Now You Know
the Secrets

Hey, you've made it all the way to the last chapter! If you're motivated enough to have read this far, you're certainly motivated enough to apply what you've learned and to get straight A's.

The importance of a comprehensive, systematic, methodical approach to study cannot be overstated. It's the key to my straight A's, and it will be the key to yours. To get good grades consistently, you've got to be consistent and thorough in the way you study. You can't take a haphazard approach to college—unless you're looking for haphazard results.

Let's spend some time briefly reviewing the main points from each chapter. If anything doesn't sound familiar, you'd better go back and read the appropriate chapter again. In fact, taking a quick look through the whole book again is probably a good idea. But for those who don't, this review will provide a summary of its main points.

IF I CAN DO IT, SO CAN YOU

◆ I went from being a mediocre high school student to a straight-A college student. If I can do it, so can you. Confidence in yourself and a strong desire to do well are the keys.

- This book was written by a student, incorporating suggestions from other students; and it is full of practical advice for doing as well in college as you want to.
- Learning the rules of the "college game" and the advanced strategies I provide in this book will equip you to win the game. Thinking of college as a game may help you keep things in perspective and reduce your level of stress.
- Good grades can bring you a variety of opportunities that for many people are worth seeking.
- Reading this entire book and applying the methods described will allow you to channel your motivation into achievement of the grades you want.

YOU'RE THE BOSS ON THIS JOB

- Look at going to school as a job, and appoint yourself boss.
- Think about what you hope to get out of going to college, and use this long-term goal to help you set short- and middle-term goals.
- Be aware of the importance of college's "nongraded" activities.
- Keep school in perspective. Don't put the rest of your life on hold while you're in college.

USE NOT JUST COMMON SENSE, BUT ALL YOUR SENSES

- The more senses involved in a learning experience, the better chance the mind has of remembering it.
- Incorporate as many senses as possible into your study routine.
- Be aware of the importance of your senses of sight, hearing, and tough as you skim over your textbook reading assignments, attend lectures, take notes, rewrite notes, and chant formulas.

GIVING YOURSELF THE BEST SHOT: REGISTERING FOR CLASSES

Registering for classes each semester is a critical part of your work. While academic advisers may help you, ultimately you are the person responsible for choosing your courses. Remember, taking the right balance of classes each semester can improve your grades. Here are my general hints:

◆ Consider your long-term goal when you begin planning your semester schedule.
◆ Use all of the resources—the course catalog, course requirement lists, other students, instructors, and your academic adviser—to help you decide what you need to take and when you should take it.
◆ Consider your interests, your sleep-wake cycle, and your feelings about class size when you plan your schedule.
◆ Try to avoid loading yourself down with too many classes from any one category (Mostly Lecture, Mostly Lab Work, Mostly Reading, Mostly Writing, Mostly Homework) when you plan your semester schedule.

THE INSTRUCTOR IS YOUR MOST VALUABLE RESOURCE

Your instructors are your most valuable resource during your entire college career. I recommend the following to be sure you don't waste this resource:

◆ Research the instructors before signing up for classes. Sources of information include other students, other instructors, student government and fraternity and sorority organizations, lists of "outstanding teacher" award winners, and written student evaluations.
◆ Introduce yourself to your instructors early in the semester. Let them know why you're taking their class and that you want and plan to do well.
◆ Use office hours and extra study sessions to get help with homework assignments and to have questions from lectures or your readings answered. Follow my tips for preparing for such sessions.
◆ Realize that it's your responsibility to be sure you understand and meet the requirements of the instructor's contract for an A.

CLASSMATES PROVIDE COMPETITION AND COMPANIONSHIP

Although classmates compete with you for top grades, a friendly relationship with at least one other student can do a lot for your motivation. Remember these tips:

- Classmates can help you with difficult concepts and serve as important sources of lecture notes, old exams, and nonofficial information about classes and instructors. Participating in study groups may help you study more effectively.
- Avoid students who are just looking for a free tutor or someone with whom to complain about the unfairness of life. Don't sink with their ship.
- Associate with students who challenge you to reach higher.

LET'S GO TO CLASS

What you do before, during, and after classes is critical to reaching your goal of straight A's. My advice boils down to this:

- Get your textbooks a week ahead of time so that you can preview the first week of lecture material.
- Go to campus the day before classes begin and locate all your classrooms.
- Never miss a class, get there early, and sit at the front of the room.
- Preview lecture material by reading class handouts and skimming the textbook assignments for three classes ahead of time.
- Ask questions, and be an active participant in class.
- Take complete notes. Even if you don't understand every detail of the lecture, get everything written down.
- Rewrite your notes, filling in any gaps by talking to other students or finding information in the textbook. Then reorder the notes logically.
- Make a set of condensed notes after every class by pulling key concepts, terms, tables, or graphs from your class notes.

MAKING A PEARL FROM AN IRRITATION: STUDYING EFFECTIVELY

The amount of time you spend studying is less important than *how* you study. In this chapter, I suggested the following:

- Use the "three-day-back, one-day-ahead" study method.
- Stay ahead in all your classes—never fall behind.

◆ Do all homework problems, even if they're not graded, and include them in your review sessions.

◆ View class handouts as a clear indication of what the instructor sees as important material.

◆ Temper your use of the textbook according to how valuable a source of exam questions it seems to be. In general, use it to preview lecture material, to provide a different perspective on information, and to fill in gaps in your notes.

◆ Fine old exams early in the semester, and use them to tailor your studying.

◆ Get the biggest portion of your studying out of the way in the morning, and do it in a place that is quiet and well-lighted.

◆ Take frequent short study breaks, but be sure your ten-minute break doesn't turn into twenty minutes.

◆ Be sure to do your reviews every day, and review old material before beginning homework assignments or previewing lecture material.

HITTING THE TARGET: TAILORING YOUR STUDY TO SPECIFIC COURSES

The general study tips I've provided in other chapters can be applied to all course work, but special techniques may help you do better in particular courses. Begin by categorizing your classes as *Mostly Writing, Mostly Reading, Mostly Homework, Mostly Lecture,* or *Mostly Lab Work.* Then apply the following specific study tips to each category in order to tailor your studying to the demands of courses in that category.

◆ For Mostly Writing courses, start thinking immediately about each assigned paper with regard to its topic, sources, and structure. Begin laying the groundwork for each paper as soon as possible, and plan on finishing each paper well before the due date. Seek help from the instructor or the campus writing center early in the course if you feel you'll have trouble.

◆ For Mostly Lecture courses, attend lectures, take good notes, and review your notes (Chapters 7 and 8).

◆ For Mostly Lab Work courses, read the lab material before the class. Create an outline in diagram form—a sketch of the lab procedure. Try to capture the theory behind the experiment and the significance of and reason for performing each step along the way. Stay until the class is over, and use the lab time wisely. Select your lab partner carefully.

◆ For Mostly Homework courses, read over textbook material relating to the next lecture. Always do all the homework. Do additional problems not assigned in order to give you more practice with difficult material. Review homework in the same manner as lecture notes: Review two or three past problem sets each day.

◆ For Mostly Reading courses, read, read, and read. Attend every lecture. You have to learn to make sense of what you read and to analyze and evaluate it; listen carefully to the instructor for this kind of information. Take good notes, and review them often. If you find yourself floundering in your first nontextbook reading class, ask the instructor for help.

TIME WAITS FOR NO STUDENT: SAMPLE STUDY SCHEDULE AND A GUIDE TO MANAGING YOUR TIME

Time is limited—there's no doubt about that. But the disciplined study habits you'll acquire by using a study schedule create extra time. Here's a quick recap of my suggestions for managing your time:

◆ Use a calendar to keep track of all assignment due dates and exam dates.

◆ Write a list of your study goals every evening based on homework and reading assignments, papers and lab preparations, and upcoming exams.

◆ Refer to the study list throughout your day, and try to cross of every item by the end of the day.

◆ Use every available slot of time during your workday to complete the items on your list.

◆ Don't spend more than fifteen–twenty minutes on your note reviews for each subject.

◆ Be creative in putting odd moments of time to good use.

The sample study schedule I presented in this chapter—which seems, at first glance, to entail an impossible amount of work—keeps you up to date in all your classes, prevents you from having a truly impossible amount of work to do late in the semester, and provides you with extra opportunities for interacting with instructors. It is an excellent way to learn.

THE RELATIVITY OF GRADES

To get the grades you want, you must know exactly what the instructor expects of you and how the instructor's grading system works.

◆ Use the instructor's statement of the course requirements and the "recipe" for the final grade as a guide to help you set your short-term and long-term goals for the course.
◆ Be aware that it's your responsibility to be sure you understand what you need to do to get an A in the course.
◆ Keep track of your progress in all your classes, and work to improve your performance immediately if your grades begin to slip.
◆ Remember to work hardest in the areas you're least comfortable with.
◆ Work not simply to meet but to exceed the instructor's expectations for an A student.
◆ Don't drop classes too casually, but if you do decide to drop a class, do it early in the semester so that your withdrawal won't be recorded on your transcript.

WHILE OTHERS SWEAT (OR, SEVEN DAYS BEFORE THE EXAM)

If you use the study methods presented in this book, you will be away ahead of your classmates by exam time, but there are some things you can do during the last week to increase that distance. For one thing, keep going to class, and—unless you've been told it will not be on the exam—spend 70 percent of your study time mastering the material presented during the final week before the exam.

Then, spend the other 30 percent of your study time as follows:

1. Review your original, noncondensed lecture notes at least once.
2. Review all old homework assignments.
3. Review all available old exams.
4. Look over any assigned reading material.
5. Early in the last week before the exam, ask the instructor any questions you haven't been able to answer on your own.
6. Don't spend a disproportionate amount of time studying material you already know.
7. Attend all practice, review, or question sessions.

8. Take off the night, or even the afternoon, before the exam and relax.

NO MAN—OR WOMAN—IS AN ISLAND UNTIL IT'S TIME FOR AN EXAM

◆ Use my three-pass method for attacking exams: (1) Spend ten–fifteen minutes reading through the whole exam and answering the easy questions, (2) go through it again, answering the questions with the highest point value first, and (3) if you have time, make a third pass through the exam to check your answers.
◆ Tailor your exam-taking strategy to the specific type of exam.
◆ Don't try to read too much into exam questions; keep your interpretations simple and direct. When you are confused, ask for clarification.
◆ *Never, never* leave a question unanswered. Put *something* down for every question, especially multiple-choice questions. Even if you don't have a clue as to the real answer, make an effort. If nothing else, the teacher may give you credit for effort—or for entertainment.
◆ Watch for the special pitfalls in multiple-choice exams, especially those that use Scan Tron sheets.
◆ Use dimensional analysis (flip-flops) to answer questions requiring conversion from one unit of measurement to another.
◆ Use estimates to check your answers to math questions.
◆ Approach essay exams as follows: Outline the main points you wish to cover, and then order them logically. Your first paragraph should contain a restatement of the question and your thesis. Support your thesis with the logically ordered points. Conclude with a complete but brief summary of these points. Keep your essay direct and to the point. Proofread the whole essay.

If you use the study methods presented in this book, you will know the exam material well; and if you use the exam methods, you will provide good, clear answers to questions and finish on time, all of which will maximize your score.

GOING TO SCHOOL PART-TIME

One of the most obvious solutions to the problem of not having enough money to go to college is to work part-time or full-time and go to school part-time. Getting through college on a part-time basis presents special challenges, and in this chapter I provided some tips for meeting those challenges.

◆ Set educational goals, and use these goals to devise a plan for getting through college.
◆ Don't overextend yourself!
◆ Use my sample plan to decide on the number of credit hours to take in one semester.
◆ Take steps to compensate for being out of the information loop: Stay in touch with your academic adviser, make friends with your classmates, and read the student newspaper.
◆ Be aware that you may have trouble scheduling required classes, and be creative in overcoming that difficulty.

STUDENT STRESS

The best defense against stress is a good offense. Recognize the warning signs and the sources of stress in your life, and take steps to deal with them before they deal with you. Let's review my tips for alleviating stress.

◆ Learn to recognize it.
◆ Determining where you are in the student stress cycle is a good first step toward breaking the stress cycle.
◆ Apply the study methods presented in this book to help you organize your life and keep up to date in all your classes.
◆ Participate regularly in some sort of activity that releases stress, one that requires concentration and provides aerobic exercise.
◆ Seek help when you're feeling really stressed, anxious, or depressed.
◆ Avoid getting caught up in too many extracurricular activities.
◆ Get adequate rest, and eat a balanced diet.
◆ Use stress to your advantage when possible.
◆ Reevaluate your goals, and drop back if necessary.
◆ Assess your overall happiness frequently.
◆ Try various relaxation techniques to help manage stress.
◆ Don't let substance abuse ruin your academic career.

*　　*　　*　　*　　*

That's the review. The final question for you is this: Now that you know the secret to getting straight A's, are you willing to put forth the effort and make it work for you? You've made it through to the end of this book, so I know you have perseverance. Now put some of that stick-to-itiveness into your approach to college.

Organizing your life and motivating yourself to do well will affect more than your grades. Once you've taken charge of your life, you'll feel yourself growing in ways you never expected. You'll realize that your life is your own.

How should I end the book? The most important thing is for you to believe in yourself. I can't get good grades for you, but you can get them for yourself. These methods worked for me and for many other top students, and I know they will work for you. You know everything I know about how to do it; now it's up to you.

Special Topics

STUDENT RIGHTS

Students have the right to be treated with respect. While you may be among the lucky students who have never had to deal with this problem, it's very possible that sometime during the four years it takes to get an undergraduate degree you'll find yourself feeling ill-used. If you ever feel that you're being discriminated against, unduly harassed, or otherwise unfairly treated, be very serious and careful in your approach to the problem. Take some time to cool off and think things over. Are you overreacting? Misinterpreting something? Or is there really a problem?

If you're sure there is a problem, there are steps you can take to solve it. Most campuses have offices or centers set up specifically to deal with charges of sexual harassment or discrimination. Most colleges also have a student code, a student ombudsman, and other institutionalized mechanisms for assisting students who need help. If you want to begin to deal with the problem on your own, present your concerns and allow the instructor an opportunity to resolve the difference in a nonconfrontational manner. If it's an issue you're very uncomfortable with, you may want to take a friend along or ask another instructor to sit in on the discussion. If this approach doesn't work, and if your grade or your comfort in the classroom is in jeopardy, make an appointment to discuss the problem with the department head or, if more drastic measures are warranted, the dean. Don't be shy; this is one of the many jobs delegated to these administrators. You may be surprised to find the dean more than willing to discuss the problem and work with you and your instructor to resolve it. You may also find that you are not the only student who has complained about this particular instructor; by adding your name to a growing list, you may be helping ensure that something will be done to solve the problem.

While an occasional disagreement is sure to arise, serious conflicts with instructors rarely do. But I wanted to address the point because throughout your college years, you will take classes from many instructors with whom you will spend countless hours. Through these many encounters, there is a good possibility that at least once you'll find yourself in the uncomfortable position of feeling that your rights as a student (and a human being) have been violated. I encourage you to stand up for yourself. To do any less than this can lead to a loss of pride and self-confidence, which can affect your performance in school—and, potentially, in life.

WHEN YOU AND YOUR INSTRUCTOR DISAGREE ABOUT GRADES

If you feel you have been dealt with unfairly with regard to classroom assignments, exams, or your final grade, I recommend that you take at least a day to cool off and consider the circumstances and your preparedness as objectively as possible. Sometimes the problem is a simple one. Instructors are human, and it may be that they copied a final grade incorrectly or made a mistake adding up the grades for the semester. But in other cases, it may be a matter of a difference of opinion; you feel your work on an assignment, or your answer on an exam, was worth a higher grade than your instructor does. Again, think things through carefully before acting.

If, after this period of reflection, you feel the same way and are confident in your argument, approach your instructor after class to set up an appointment to discuss the matter. Most teachers welcome students' input on grading and will admit openly that mistakes are occasionally made.

Before you talk to the instructor, however, carefully check the grades you received from every homework assignment and test given by this instructor. If you've been keeping your personal scorecard, you should have a very good idea of your progress in the class—and it's critical to find out why the instructor has a different view. If you've been conscientious in learning from your mistakes and have improved your grade on each succeeding assignment, you have a much better position from which to discuss the matter.

Should the teacher reject your claim and you still feel the grade is unfair, you have the right to make an appointment with the department head or the dean of students to discuss the problem. I recommend this step only if the problem has occurred repeatedly and your final grade in the class is in jeopardy. Once you initiate contact with the dean, you may find yourself with an uncomfortable barrier between you and the instructor. No matter the outcome, you both lose something—and, in your case, that might mean the difference between an A and a B.

TIPS FOR COMMUTERS

Commuting students face some of the same problems that part-time students do, and I recommend that they read the chapter on going to school part-time, particularly the section on being out of the information loop. A few other study tips may be especially useful to commuters.

1. Consider taping lectures in the classes you feel you'll need the most study time for and then listening to the lecture tapes while you drive. Even if you're unable to pay attention all the time, you'll be surprised at how much of the information seeps into your brain through this relatively painless process. Beware, however, of a tendency to sleep through lectures because you know they're being taped. You need to hear it in class first and then use the tape for review only.
2. Try to find a classmate who's interested in car pooling—and then spend the time in the car going over your lecture notes, quizzing each other, or discussing ideas for term papers.
3. Because you won't have a dorm room to return to between classes, you may need to be creative to find places to work and study. Consider the library and empty seminar rooms or lecture halls. As long as the weather cooperates, you may find that your car is a comfortable, quiet, and private study nook.
4. As a commuter, pay particular attention to my advice to study at every available opportunity during the day. You probably have to spend more of your time than a dorm student does on activities such as purchasing and preparing food. (Another thing you might want to consider is purchasing meal tickets to eat on campus—but

be sure to get a review of the quality of meals before you spend any money!)

5. Consider attending lectures, concerts, and seminars on campus and joining an organization related to your major to help overcome the problem of being out of the information loop.

EXTRA HELP FOR EVERYONE

One of the best-kept secrets on college campuses is all the extra help that's available for students. Writing centers, study skills centers, career planning workshops, tutoring centers, counseling services—it's amazing how many resources there are. Actually, it's not a secret; it's usually spelled out pretty clearly in the college catalog, brochures, posters on bulletin boards, and so on. But for some reason, students rarely pay attention to these kinds of announcements.

And let me say this right away: It's not only students who are failing all their classes and about to be thrown out of school who can use these resources. They're open to all students, and the more use you make of them, the better you're likely to do. In fact, most students who are doing poorly are probably not motivated enough to walk over to the right building and ask for help. You want to do well? Get all the extra help you can.

I found the tutorial center at my school particularly valuable my first two semesters. Subjects like math, chemistry, and English composition were all new to me, and the one hour of lecture three times a week just didn't seem to be enough. Every night when I tried to do the homework assignments, I would run into problems—brick walls— that would lead to hours of frustration. For me, the answer was the tutorial center.

Most tutorial centers are staffed by students who are just a little further along in the educational process than those they tutor. These students can help you work through difficult homework problems, give you helpful study hints, and proofread and make suggestions on term papers. Some centers require a usage fee; others are free (well, paid for through your tuition or your activities fee). At some schools, tutoring may be available through individual departments.

Are you still undecided about your major and your career plans? Campus career counseling centers are stocked with valuable resource materials and staffed by people trained to help you make these decisions. Worried about your study or test-taking strategies? Go to the campus study skills center and make use of the books, workshops, and personnel there.

Nervous about your writing skills? Make use of the writing centers most colleges have. In addition to workshops, classes, and training sessions on various aspects of writing, these centers usually offer staff members who will work personally with you on your writing assignments for various classes. Why not increase your changes for an A on your economics term paper if you can? And writing is a skill you'll need for many classes and throughout life.

Still stuck in the student stress cycle I described in Chapter 15? Having trouble recovering from your girlfriend's sudden departure from your life? Feeling really depressed about life in general? Avail yourself of the school's counseling services. Talk to a trained psychologist or a peer counselor. Unless you have a pretty great insurance plan later in life, this is probably the only time you'll be able to get this kind of counseling absolutely free.

Nobody said college would be easy, and you may encounter a variety of problems. But don't let those problems overwhelm you and throw you off track. You're not alone; there's help out there.

EXTRA-CREDIT WORK

I've found that extra-credit work is usually offered in one of two ways: (1) The instructor includes a description of what kind of extra-credit work may be done, and its contribution to your final grade, in the original list of course requirements or (2) the instructor offers an opportunity to do extra-credit work late in the semester because many students in the class are doing poorly. (In a way, this latter type is just another form of a curve—if everyone does the extra-credit work and gets full credit for it, everyone's grades will be pulled up by the same amount. But there's always a chance that not all students will do the work, and that not all who try will complete the work satisfactorily. It's definitely to your advantage to give it a shot.)

In my opinion, you're a foot not to take advantage of any opportunity to do extra-credit work—and to do it early in the semester, if it's offered, and do it well. The most obvious reason for doing it is as added insurance that you'll get an A for the course. Many students won't both to do extra-credit work if they feel that they're pushed for time, or if they feel they're doing as well in the class as they want to. (If many students don't do homework that's assigned, imagine how many don't do extra-credit work.) Doing extra-credit work also helps demonstrate to the instructor that you're serious about the class and about getting good grades. What kind of message are you sending if you tell an instructor you want to do well in the class and then don't even attempt the extra-credit work? Doing it puts you ahead of the rest of the class. But another good reason is that extra-credit work often provides a chance to do something more creative and more interesting than the usual class assignments, a chance to learn in more depth or from another perspective. And it also may give the instructor something special to say about you if you ask for a letter of recommendation.

FINANCIAL AID AND BEYOND

For many students, the financial aid office is one of the most important resources a campus offers. Chapter 14 addresses going to college part-time, one of the options for students who have money problems and have to work full-time. Another option for students who are supporting themselves or paying for their own education is to cut their weekly workload back from forty hours and supplement their income with student loans, grants, or scholarships. Financial aid offices are set up with the specific purpose of helping needy students obtain money so that they can pursue their educations. Visit the financial aid office on your campus, and get to know the financial aid officer.

Who qualifies for financial aid? This is a complicated question that can be best answered by your particular campus officer. I talked to some financial aid counselors while I was working on this book, and they agreed that the best advice is for students and parents to get all the up-to-date information they can on scholarships, grants, loans, and work programs from high school guidance counselors and college financial aid officers. Details change so frequently that it would be useless for me to try to give you more specific advice. But here, as elsewhere in this book, you're the boss; and you'd do well to arm yourself with as much help and information as possible before giving up on the idea of going to college because it costs too much.

If you're struggling to balance work and school, consider the following sources of help: Federally funded student loans may allow you to defer repayment while you're attending college; and when you *do* start paying back, the interest rate is quite reasonable. There are also grants and scholarships that in most cases do not need to be repaid. Good grades can save you money; investigate the competitive scholarships and awards available from the alumni association or from particular college departments. If the top student in computer science wins a $500 award, isn't it worth a little extra studying to be that top student?

This may differ at different schools, but usually as long as you're taking at least six units (credit hours), you should have loan, grant, and scholarship money available to you. Once your enrollment drops below six units (credit hours), you change to half-time enrollment status, and the aid available to you is significantly reduced.

Remember that old saying about the squeaky wheel always getting the grease? This is really true of college financial aid. There are thousands of students on campuses across the country who feel that they have legitimate need for the resources of their financial aid offices, and you have to compete with them. Be persistent! Document your need. Visit the financial aid office until you get the information you need. Be a squeaky wheel.

And remember that early bird who always gets the worm? This also applies to college financial aid. The amount of money available in the form of loans, grants, and scholarships is limited, so get your application in early, and never miss a filing deadline. For many financial aid applications, the deadline is April 1.

Finally, be creative! Look for money to finance your college education where others do not. Many colleges have scholarship money that goes unclaimed every year because students did not take the time to search it out and fill out the necessary paperwork. A creative place to look for scholarship money is your parents' (or your own) employer. There is usually much less competition for these scholarships. One combination of work and school that works well is to seek full-time employment at a college or university that allows its staff to attend classes without paying tuition. Or check with your employer to see if there are any programs through which the costs of your education would be paid by the company you work for. Other sources to investigate are local clubs and organizations such as Rotary Club.

School services and opportunities can cut costs for you, too. When you pay your tuition, it doesn't go solely toward your classes. Many students don't realize that they are part of a huge buying group that makes available to them many opportunities and services they might otherwise have difficulty obtaining. As with financial aid, however, you may have to search out such services.

For example, many colleges have health care and dental programs available to students at a greatly reduced cost. This may be particularly true at schools with medical and dental school programs. You may have to be a med student's guinea pig to qualify, but you'll get inexpensive, sometimes even free, health care. And speaking of guinea pigs, you may be able to *earn* money by participating in someone's research project. Watch the campus newspaper and bulletin boards for ads.

College campuses often have recreational facilities that rival those at private health clubs. Fees for these facilities are often included in college tuition and available at little, if any, additional cost. And don't forget entertainment; you usually can get into plays, movies, museums, and sports events for less if you are a student.

As a student, you're never alone. There are usually thousands of others with needs similar to yours. For example, if you are a single parent struggling to pursue your education while playing super parent, you might benefit from searching out other single parents going through the same thing. Find out how they're coping and what services they have found to assist them. Some innovative colleges have arranged campus child care for parents so that they can make the most of their educational opportunities; talking to other parents will help you find out whether such services exist at your school.

Whatever your particular needs, don't let it keep you from getting a college education—if that's what you really want. Help is available in a variety of forms; all you have to do is find it.

INDEX